NATIONAL ECONOMIC POLICY

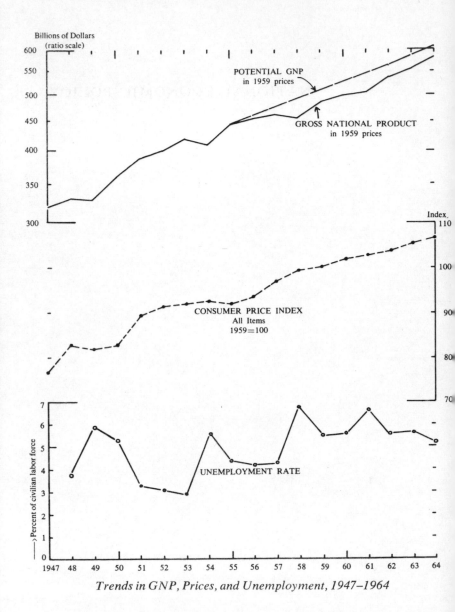

Trends in GNP, Prices, and Unemployment, 1947–1964

NATIONAL ECONOMIC POLICY

ESSAYS

BY JAMES TOBIN

New Haven and London

Yale University Press

1966

Copyright © 1966 by Yale University.
Designed by Sally Sullivan,
set in Times Roman type,
and printed in the United States of America by
The Carl Purington Rollins Printing-Office
of Yale University Press.
Distributed in Canada by McGill University Press.
All rights reserved. This book may not be
reproduced, in whole or in part, in any form
(except by reviewers for the public press),
without written permission from the publishers.
Library of Congress catalog card number: 66–12514

To the memory of my father
Louis Michael Tobin 1879–1944

Preface

Collected in this volume are eighteen essays I have written on national economic policy during the past fifteen years. Most of them were addressed to a general audience, not just to the economics profession. Most of them were evoked by events or controversies of the time, and express with considerable emphasis a definite point of view.

I hope that economic fact and logic play some part in the arguments, but they can obviously bear only part of the weight of the conclusions advocated. These depend also on the social values, or prejudices, of the author. I do not apologize for these, but merely point out that I wrote these essays as a concerned citizen, a political animal as well as a professional economist.

If there is a unifying theme to the positions taken on diverse subjects, it is simply a reminder that the whole purpose of the economy is production of goods or services for consumption now or in the future. I think the burden of proof should always be on those who would produce less rather than more, on those who would leave idle men or machines or land that could be used. It is amazing how many reasons can be found to justify such waste: fears of inflation, balance-of-payments deficits, unbalanced budgets, excessive national debt, loss of confidence in the dollar, etc., etc. This catalogue of financial shibboleths and taboos scares the confused layman out of a commonsense, pragmatic approach to economic policy. The veil of money obscures the simple and basic problem of any society: to what uses to allocate its labor and other productive resources to get the most out of them. Surely no one would allocate them to idleness. Perhaps price stability, fixed exchange rates, balanced budgets, and the like can be justified as means to achieving and sustaining high employment, production, and consumption. Too often the means are accorded precedence over the end, and I am led to take up my pen to defend the basic objective of economic policy against its spurious rivals.

The papers are reprinted here as they appeared originally, except for the elimination of avoidable repetition. They doubtless reveal some inconsistencies, and probably I would not today write a single essay exactly the same way again. But I stand by the general point of view.

I thank the efficient office staff of the Cowles Foundation at Yale, in particular Miss Althea Strauss and Mrs. Laura Harrison, for helping me meet the original deadlines for these articles. I am grateful to Mrs. Karen Hester for editorial assistance in preparing the essays for publication in this form. I owe a large debt to my teachers and fellow students at Harvard, my colleagues and students at Yale, and my associates in Washington. But I will not implicate any of them by name.

James Tobin

New Haven
July 1965

Contents

Preface   vii

PART I. GOVERNMENT AND THE ECONOMY   1
Introduction   3
1   How Planned Is Our Economy?   5
2   The Frontier Between Business and Government   15
3   Barry's Economic Crusade   25
4   The New Era of Good Feeling Between Business
        and Government   35

PART II. FISCAL POLICY, THE BUDGET,
        AND GROWTH   43
Introduction   45
5   Deficit, Deficit, Who's Got the Deficit?   49
6   Defense, Dollars, and Doctrines   56
7   On the Economic Burden of Defense   70
8   Growth Through Taxation   78
9   Economic Growth as an Objective of
        Government Policy   89

PART III. MONETARY POLICY AND INFLATION   115
Introduction   117
10   Monetary Restriction and Direct Controls   123
11   Labor and Economic Stabilization   128
12   The Future of the Fed   134
13   Lessons of Monetary History   144

PART IV. THE INTERNATIONAL
    MONETARY SYSTEM   149

Introduction   151

14   Europe and the Dollar   153

15   Economic Progress and the International
     Monetary System   161

16   The Problem of International Liquidity   176

17   The Future of the Dollar as International Money   186

PART V. ACADEMIC ECONOMICS IN
    WASHINGTON   199

18   Academic Economics in Washington   201

Index   207

PART I

GOVERNMENT AND THE ECONOMY

Introduction

From 1936 to 1964 American politics was dominated by a highly charged ideological debate on the proper role of the federal government in the economy. A large segment of business opinion held that the New Deal had set in motion a vast and dangerous federal invasion of private resources and private freedoms. These antigovernment feelings moderated, of course, during the explicitly pro-business Administration of President Eisenhower. But suspicion and hostility revived during the Administration of President Kennedy, reaching a fever pitch after the steel price incident and the stock market decline in the spring of 1962.

The point of the first two essays, Chapters 1 and 2, is that emotional attack on the federal government is misplaced and misinformed. Ideological contention between grand alternative "systems" is quite irrelevant in America today. Instead, the activities of government need to be debated and evaluated pragmatically case by case. I was particularly concerned to make this point in the fall of 1962. I had served in the Kennedy Administration until August of that year, and I knew the unrequited efforts that the President and his Administration had made to gain the confidence of the business and financial community.

The nomination of Barry Goldwater in 1964 drew the ideological lines more sharply than in any previous election. The essay reprinted as Chapter 3 was a campaign comment on Goldwater's crusade against federal government. Most businessmen had no heart for the uncompromising conservative line once it had captured a major party. They were willing to end their thirty years' war against the New Deal, and President Johnson was ready to welcome them to his national consensus. This is the theme sketched in Chapter 4.

Chapter 1

How Planned Is Our Economy?

For Americans of sufficient age and memory, current political debate about government and business must sound comfortably familiar. Like the New Deal and Fair Deal before it, the New Frontier has provoked shrill warnings that an "anti-business" Administration seeks to supplant the "free enterprise system" with a "planned economy." The public defenders of free enterprise, their natural hostility to government muted during eight years of Republican rule, have scarcely concealed their enthusiasm at finding Washington once again occupied by the enemy. The Kennedy Administration has been puzzled and hurt to find itself cast in this role. Unlike its Democratic predecessors, the New Frontier leaned over backward to avoid earning an "anti-business" label and to forestall suspicions that it contemplated radical changes in U.S. economic institutions. Evidently there is considerable misunderstanding—between the Administration and its critics, and in the public at large—about the role of government policies and plans in a private enterprise economy such as ours.

To what extent can and does the federal government plan and control the American economy? Has the Kennedy Administration increased, or proposed to increase, federal economic planning and control?

To answer these questions, it is essential to begin with a simple distinction, all too rarely respected in public discussion. The distinction is between *plans* and *controls*. In the contexts of everyday life, planning simply means "thinking ahead," basing current actions and decisions on rational calculation of their future consequences. In discussions of government and the economy, however, *planning* connotes to many people an elaborate regime of coercive *controls* over the daily economic behavior of business managers, workers, and consumers. There is no necessary connection between the two. Clearly there is a great difference between planning one's own actions and coercing the actions of others, between using forethought and using force.

Government controls over the activities of specific business firms and individuals—the quantities of materials they can buy and stock, the kinds and quantities of goods they can produce, the amounts they can or must sell to different customers, the prices they may or must charge, etc.—are familiar to the American people from the Second World War. No one in his right mind wishes to revive the battery of wartime controls unless another full-scale military mobilization is forced upon us.

A few controls, some federal, others state and local, are permanently scattered over the peacetime economic landscape. These are quite a mixed bag. Some, like the strengthened drug legislation recently adopted in the wake of the thalidomide scare, are meant simply to safeguard public health or safety. The rates and services of public utilities are regulated on the ground that customers of natural or government-franchised monopolies lack the automatic protection of competition. Elsewhere, some direct government interventions, like those under the antitrust laws, are intended to preserve or restore competition. Other interventions are designed to shelter producers from competition among themselves and with others—examples are agricultural price and production controls, minimum wages, "fair-trade" laws, oil production and import quotas. In short, the direct economic controls we have in peacetime serve a variety of very special purposes, or crosspurposes, and interests. They are administered by special federal and state agencies, many of which enjoy considerable autonomy. These controls are certainly not available to any federal administration as instruments of an overall economic strategy or "plan."

The Kennedy Administration's approach to special-purpose direct controls has varied pragmatically with the subject matter. If the President has favored tighter production controls over farmers in order to save federal money, he has also proposed to dismantle many government regulations restricting competition in the transportation industries.

To carry out a general policy to promote economic stability and growth, the government must rely on quite different instruments, mainly on fiscal and monetary measures. These are general, impersonal, and diffuse in their effects upon economic activity. Unlike the detailed controls of wartime, these measures do not supplant markets or prevent the forces of supply and demand from determining the prices and quantities of goods and services bought and sold. They do not work through orders to particular firms or individuals to take, or to refrain from taking, specific actions. But they do affect the general market environment in which businessmen and consumers freely make choices and decisions. For these reasons, they are sometimes called "indirect controls."

The major indirect control is the federal budget. The federal government spends over $60 billion per year to buy goods and services (11 per cent of the Gross National Product), and distributes in addition more than $45 billion in veterans' pensions, Social Security and welfare benefits, grants-in-aid to state and local governments, and other "transfer payments" for which no current productive services are rendered. Government expenditures affect first of all the economic fortunes of the individuals and businesses that actually receive the government checks. But as the initial recipients respend the money, government outlays are quickly and widely diffused over the whole country. Consequently an increase in federal expenditures, whatever its initial purpose and distribution, is an injection of general purchasing power into the economy. Just like injections of purchasing power from private sources, a rise in federal spending tends to increase sales, jobs, incomes, profits, and sometimes prices, throughout the economy. On the other side of the budget ledger, taxes drain purchasing power from the economy. Higher taxes affect first of all the taxpayers on whom they are levied. But the reduction in their ability to spend spreads to the whole economy, generally reducing sales, jobs, incomes, profits, and sometimes prices.

The budget therefore packs tremendous power for inflation or deflation, for growth or stagnation, for unemployment or full employment. This power neither vanishes if ignored nor increases if acknowledged. To plan the budget with a view to overall economic balance does not add to the government's power over the economy. It is only an attempt to exercise this power rationally rather than blindly.

In almost all advanced countries, the economic power of the budget has long since been explicitly acknowledged. In France, Germany, the United Kingdom, Holland, Sweden—to name a few countries which in other respects differ widely both economically and politically—the government budget is regarded as a major instrument of general economic planning, not simply as an accounting device to facilitate internal governmental housekeeping. In those countries the government attempts through each year's budget to achieve a balance between aggregate purchasing power and the capacity of the country to produce. The budget is consciously made tighter—higher taxes relative to expenditures—if excessive purchasing power threatens inflation or balance-of-payments difficulties. It is consciously made easier—lower taxes or higher expenditures—if deficiencies of total demand threaten to produce unemployment and excess capacity.

In our own country, unfortunately, the economic use of the government budget is only now emerging from the area of ideological controversy. Indeed it is probably anxiety over the budget —rather than any proliferation of direct controls—that is at the bottom of many current complaints about "economic planning." Some business leaders, particularly in the Committee for Economic Development, have long since joined the great majority of economists in advocating flexible budget policy. But a large segment of business opinion, and of general public opinion, regards it as heresy to frame the federal budget with any end in view except strict balance of administrative expenditures and receipts. President Eisenhower and his lieutenants repeatedly preached solemn sermons against fiscal heresy; and the evils of deficit finance were a favorite theme of the former President and of lesser Republican orators during the 1960 election campaign.

The other main "indirect control" is monetary policy. Under the Constitution the federal government has the inescapable power and responsibility of a central government "to coin money,

[and] regulate the value thereof." As the economy developed, bank checks supplanted coins and paper currency as the usual means of payment. The government therefore acquired, mainly through the Federal Reserve Act of 1913, significant control of the aggregate volume of bank deposits and bank credit. Banks are required to hold a certain percentage of their deposits as reserves, either in vault cash or on deposit with Federal Reserve Banks. The percentage required can be within limits varied by Federal Reserve authorities. More important, the "Fed" controls, principally by open-market transactions in government securities, the aggregate dollar volume of reserve assets available to the banks to satisfy the requirements. These are indirect and impersonal controls. Although they decisively affect general monetary and credit conditions throughout the economy, they do not interfere with the free choices of individual banks, depositors, and borrowers or with competition among banks for deposits and loans.

Not even the most doctrinaire advocate of laissez-faire favors free enterprise in the minting of coins or the printing of paper currency; and few would argue that the quantity of bank-created money can safely be left to unfettered competition among private banks. There is no escape from the fact that the government possesses and must exercise monetary powers over the economy. Tight money restricts, and easy money encourages, private borrowing and spending. The only issue is whether these powers are to be exercised for narrowly defined monetary objectives or, in planned concert with the government's fiscal powers, for the broad objectives of economic stability and growth.

Critics who detect tendencies toward economic planning in Washington should recall the Employment Act of 1946. This Act, passed by heavy bipartisan majorities, charges the federal government to concert the various measures at its command in the interest of achieving "maximum employment, production, and purchasing power." The President and his Council of Economic Advisers are directed to keep track of trends in employment, production, and purchasing power, to compare levels actually obtaining with the "maximum" levels desired, to consider how federal policies might improve the performance of the economy, and to report to the Congress on these matters at least once a year.

With this Act as a solemn expression of national policy, no Administration, Democratic or Republican, can avoid a modest amount of economic planning. At all times—and especially when the yearly budget and legislative program are being prepared—the President, his cabinet officers and advisers, and the Federal Reserve authorities must be asking themselves: Is total demand in the economy likely to be deficient or adequate or excessive? Should the government give demand a boost, by spending more or taxing less or by an easier monetary policy? Or should demand be checked either by a tighter budget or more restrictive credit policies? Of course economic diagnosis and therapy are far from being exact sciences. There is always plenty of room for disagreement about appropriate policy. That is precisely why the Employment Act provides in the Joint Economic Committee of the Congress machinery for a critical appraisal of the President's diagnosis and recommendations.

The Kennedy Administration has proposed to sharpen the tools of fiscal and monetary management. In January 1962 the President proposed three measures to reinforce the federal government's arsenal of anti-recession weapons: (1) a procedure by which the President could make temporary uniform reductions (not exceeding five percentage points) in personal income tax rates; (2) a standby program of public capital expenditures, to be triggered by increases in unemployment; and (3) permanent improvement of unemployment insurance, including automatic lengthening of benefit periods during times of high unemployment. None of these proposals involves new government controls over individuals or businesses; none of them thrusts the government into new areas of activity. But they would greatly strengthen the government's hand in carrying out the purposes of the Employment Act. Unfortunately the Congress has not acted on any of these proposals.

Along with the central objective of the Employment Act—high employment—the Administration has emphasized two other economic objectives. One is the long-run growth of the economy, and the other is restoration of balance between the nation's international payments and receipts.

Unlike its predecessor, which was sometimes contemptuous of "growthmanship," the Kennedy Administration explicitly aims at a higher growth rate—specifically to reach $4\frac{1}{2}$ per cent per year in the '60s, compared to the $2\frac{1}{2}$ per cent realized in the years 1953–60. As one means toward this end, the Administration has sought to encourage business investment—by maintaining credit conditions as easy as international monetary conditions permit, by reforming the tax treatment of depreciation, and by offering a 7 per cent credit against taxes for expenditures for new equipment. Some purists, both liberal and conservative, have objected to using the tax system to stimulate investment. But their purism seems misplaced if it means that a tax structure shot through with loopholes that serve narrow private ends should not be adapted to serve a ranking national objective. At any rate, these measures can scarcely be described as "anti-business."

The Administration's interest in growth does not mean new controls over businesses or individuals. No one is to be ordered to grow! All that the growth orientation implies is a somewhat different emphasis in the use of traditional instruments of policy —the budget, the tax structure, and monetary control.

At the same time, more explicit long-range economic planning, both public and private, may help to promote economic growth. France has found it useful for the government to cooperate with business and labor in projecting the French economy ahead for four or five years. The French plan indicates a feasible rate of growth for the economy as a whole ($5\frac{1}{2}$ per cent per year under the Fourth Plan, for 1961–65), together with corresponding estimates of the growth of major sectors, public and private. These estimates are in no sense compulsory. But they give French businessmen valuable guidance and mutual confidence. Each industry can make the investments that growth requires with some assurance that similar investments by others will expand its markets. A somewhat similar exercise by the Committee for Economic Development in 1943, *Markets After the War,* helped to raise the sights of American businessmen to the unprecedented levels of peacetime demand of which a prosperous American economy was capable. The Conservative government in Britain, in the hope of raising Britain's sluggish growth rate, is importing some French planning procedures. Development of cooperation and trust between government, business, and labor in the United States may some day permit similar procedures—which involve no government controls—to be used in promoting steadier and faster economic expansion in this country.

The Administration's efforts to restore balance-of-payments equilibrium, like its policies to promote economic growth, have employed conventional tools. No new controls or restriction of transactions inside or outside the country have been imposed or requested. Spurred by the gold problem, the Administration proposed, with limited success in the Congress, to eliminate outmoded tax incentives for investment in other advanced countries. And the Federal Reserve and the Treasury have managed bank reserves and the federal debt somewhat differently than if their only concerns were the domestic economy. For example, the Federal Reserve early in 1961 abandoned its "bills only" policy of the Eisenhower years, and late in 1962 permitted banks to offer higher interest rates on time and savings deposits. Both moves were attempts to reconcile the need to hold short-term funds in the country with the credit requirements of domestic expansion.

In summary, the Kennedy Administration has not asked for new controls. It does not seek to add to the coercive powers of government over the economic actions of individual citizens. But it has taken seriously the broad responsibility of the federal government, under the Employment Act of 1946, for economic prosperity and growth. The Administration has tried to define, perhaps more explicitly than its predecessor, objectives and prospects for the U.S. economy as a whole. The federal government inevitably has a tremendous influence upon the economy, as the nation's biggest customer, employer, tax collector, and borrower, and as the ultimate source and regulator of money and credit. The present Administration is committed—again perhaps more strongly than its predecessor—to directing the economic influence of the federal government to the achievement of national economic goals, including long-run economic growth. This commitment does not involve any new instruments of economic control. But it may well involve more planning, in the simple everyday meaning of thinking ahead.

But what about steel prices? Does that dramatic episode not prove that the Administration seeks to substitute government controls for private decisions? It proves, if anything, the opposite, for the Administration's actions were part of a determined effort to defend the dollar *without* new controls.

Ever since the war, pressures for wage and price increases, arising from concentrations of wage- and price-making power in unions and corporations, have been a major problem in all democratic industrial countries. Indirect controls, i.e. restrictive monetary and fiscal measures, can eliminate these pressures, if at all, only at heavy costs in unemployment and underproduction. In some countries, notably Holland, the answer to this cruel dilemma has been government control of wages and prices. This is certainly an unacceptable solution for the United States. But in the face of serious balance-of-payments difficulties, the U.S. cannot afford new twists of the wage–price spiral. For this reason, both President Eisenhower and President Kennedy have tried to throw the moral weight of the presidency and of public opinion on the side of restraint in wage negotiations and price decisions. Whatever their disagreements on other matters, the Councils of Economic Advisers of the two presidents have agreed on the principles of noninflationary wage and price behavior.

The government has been involved, one way or another, in every labor–management dispute and settlement in steel since the war. No administration can regard a stoppage in so basic an industry as a purely private concern to which the government is indifferent. Vice-President Nixon and other officers of the Eisenhower Administration arranged the settlement that ended the 116-day steel strike of 1959. The settlement reached in early 1960 involved a 3.7 per cent per year increase in hourly employment costs but was accompanied by no price increase. In 1963 the Kennedy Administration sought to encourage the parties to reach a new steel labor contract without a strike well before the June 30 deadline. But, as the President had made clear to everyone as early as the previous September, the Administration did not seek peace at any price level. The President and Secretary Goldberg sought a noninflationary settlement, holding the wage increase within the range of productivity gains in order to permit stability in steel prices. It was a fair assumption that the 1962 settlement met this test—the increase in hourly employment costs, 2½ per cent per year, was the most moderate since the war. The ink was scarcely dry on the new contracts when U.S. Steel precipitated the famous events of April 10–13. After using his moral influence to obtain moderation from the union, the President could scarcely have failed to speak out against the announced price increase.

The great issues that aroused the ideological battalions in the past are not very relevant today. Plenty of issues remain. But they are not for the most part questions of widening or narrowing the sphere of government activity. Rather they are differences of view about national priorities among various government activities —defense, space, education, etc.—and between public and private uses of economic resources. Or they concern the best use of existing government powers to achieve full employment, stability, and economic progress. It is not surprising that many observers differ with the Kennedy Administration's policies and proposals. What is surprising, in the 1960s, is that some critics have regarded the Administration's economic program—and sometimes the very fact that it has a program—as an occasion for summoning the troops to a new antigovernment crusade. For surely it is a proper concern of the government whether the economy is in recession or prosperity, whether unemployment is 7 per cent or 4 per cent of the labor force, whether prices are rising or reasonably stable, whether the dollar is weak or strong abroad, whether Gross National Product is $500 or $570 or $600 billion, and whether GNP is on average growing at 2½ or 4½ per cent per year. If conscious and coherent policy to discharge these responsibilities is "planning," then the Administration is guilty.

Chapter 2

The Frontier Between Business and Government

Business attitudes toward the New Frontier have frequently been suspicious and hostile. Evidently many businessmen believe that the frontier where the Kennedy Administration wishes to advance is the frontier between government and business. My thesis here is a simple one. These fears are misplaced. The frontier between government and business in the United States is in reality static and quiet—very possibly as inactive as at any time in the twentieth century. The defensive outcries from the business side of this frontier seem to me an obsolete ideological reflex, to which businessmen became conditioned in the days of the New Deal and Fair Deal.

What is the frontier in our society between government and business, and why do I say it is relatively quiet? There are a number of ways in which to describe the way a society divides economic activities between governmental agencies and private individuals and institutions. I cannot attempt to be exhaustive, but I propose to discuss four of these: first, the lists of economic activities assigned to public and private initiative, respectively; second, the relative magnitudes of public and private productive activity; third, governmental interventions affecting the balance of economic power and the distribution of income and wealth; and finally, the relative magnitudes of public and private uses of the fruits of economic activity.[1]

1. A fifth dimension, the scope of direct governmental regulation of private economic activities, is discussed in Chapter 1.

Originally published in *Papers of the Tenth Annual Conference on the Economic Outlook* (Ann Arbor, University of Michigan Department of Economics, November 1962).

On all these points except the last I contend that the United States exhibits today a remarkable degree of social consensus. The last item is clearly a controversial area, where there are natural and healthy divergences of interest and opinion. But the issues are greatly misunderstood, and rational discussion of them is impeded by identifying them with the great classical ideological issues of government versus private enterprise.

I. The first of my four items is qualitative rather than quantitative. It consists simply in listing in one column those economic activities carried out by government and in another those left to private individuals and organizations. I recognize, of course, that no classification can be clear-cut. Some activities (e.g. in this country the production of electric power) are shared, and some institutions are hybrid mixtures of public and private ownership and management. But in any case, I am certainly not going to try to fill those two hypothetical columns tonight. I will simply make three observations.

First, the public list is naturally much shorter in this country than in the Soviet Union or Yugoslavia. It is also shorter than the corresponding lists in most democratic industrial countries, including countries like Switzerland and Germany which are generally considered citadels of private enterprise. More activities are owned and operated by the state in those countries than in the United States; consider, for example, the fields of transportation, communication, power, and culture.

Second, comparison with other democratic industrial countries does not entitle us to claim that the way we happen to have assigned activities in this country is obviously superior. This caution applies whether we look at the efficiency and quality of the particular services involved or at the dynamism and progress of whole economies. It should not be difficult to convince anyone who has enjoyed or suffered railroad service in continental Europe, in Britain, and in the United States east and west of the Mississippi that neither public nor private ownership guarantees either good or poor service. Nor can anyone observing the overall economic progress of, say, Italy, France, Germany, Japan, Britain, and the U.S. in recent years plausibly argue that one way of assigning activities always produces better overall economic results than another.

The third observation returns me to my central theme. Whatever may be the merits or demerits of the assignment of activities that has evolved in the United States, no one is seriously trying to alter it today. Nationalization of industry is not a live issue in this country. (Indeed it is quite generally a dead issue in the Western world—even the British Labor Party is no longer very keen on further nationalization.) It was not always thus. After the First World War, permanent nationalization of the railroads was very much a live question. It is not a serious proposal today in spite of the difficulties now confronting our private carriers. In the 'twenties, our country faced the question how to organize a new activity, radio broadcasting, of which the government controlled the basic resource, the air waves. National ownership and operation of broadcasting facilities, following the pattern of other countries, was a serious possibility. Today a Democratic Administration, faced with a similar question, has entrusted communications satellites to private enterprise. After the banking collapse of the early 'thirties, nationalization of commercial banking was a serious, and not wholly implausible, possibility. Today the government is for all intents and purposes abandoning the postal savings business. When I was a high-school debater, much heat was exchanged on the question whether in principle the electric power industry should be publicly or privately owned. We now have a mixed system, and it is a rare extremist who would argue that the industry should be all private or all public. I know there are still plenty of issues and conflicts here, but they are mostly marginal and local and are therefore subject to pragmatic compromise settlement. I certainly don't see the battalions of George Norris in the present political scene. On the other side, there are perhaps a few radicals of the Right who would like to "privatize" the post office, or abolish the public schools, or sell the national parks and forests. Fortunately they command no more hearing than they deserve.

I conclude, therefore, that this sector of the public–private frontier is quiescent, that a very considerable social consensus supports the present assignment of activities. When I hear speakers pour forth rhetoric about the great battle between socialism and capitalism, when some of my business friends taunt me with bumper stickers "HELP KENNEDY stamp out free enterprise," I wonder if they are talking about the same society and age that I am living in.

"What about Medicare?" you may properly ask. The Administration's proposal does, it is true, involve a reassignment of activities. I do not propose to discuss its merits. I would only point out that, viewed in perspective, the proposed reassignment is a relatively minor one. Let us be clear about which activities it involves. Not the provision of physicians' care, or even of accommodation in hospitals and nursing homes—these are to be left in private hands, to exactly the same extent as now. It is the insurance function, and that alone, that is added to the government list—and not deleted from the private column, at that. As is most always the case, the proposed addition to the government list is a function in which private activity is not extensive, and important needs are felt to be inadequately met. Moreover, insurance of certain hazards of old age has been on the government list since the Social Security Act of 1935. That Act was widely attacked as the entering wedge for socialism, but the flourishing state of private retirement plans and life insurance companies suggests that the warnings were somewhat exaggerated, even for the private activities most directly concerned. "Medicare" is the exception that proves my general thesis. If this minor change in the two lists is the only concrete question on which can be focused the emotion and ideology surrounding the grand alternatives of socialism and capitalism, then clearly those alternatives do not today present America with any great divisive issue.

II. So much for the qualitative division of economic activity between public and private spheres. What about the quantitative magnitudes of the two spheres? How much of the nation's total economic activity does the government list account for? Has this proportion been growing? Please note that I am now talking about the locus of *origin* of national product, not the uses or *destinations* of national product. Thus for my present purpose, postal service counts as public even though it is privately purchased and consumed. And production of aircraft is private even though it is purchased by the Department of Defense. The other question—the share of government in the uses of output—is the fourth item on my list, and I shall turn to it later.

Those who are accustomed to hearing about Big and Growing Government will be surprised to learn that the share of Gross National Product, measured in constant dollars (1954 prices), originating in civilian activities of government—Federal, state, and local, including government enterprises—rose from 6 per cent in 1929 to 6½ per cent in 1961. Moreover, if 1961 had been as prosperous a year as 1929, GNP would have been at least 8 per cent higher and the civilian government share the same as in 1929, 6 per cent. Of course if we add defense production (i.e. the part "produced" by the Government itself—largely the pay of military and civilian defense personnel—and not of course defense purchases from private business), the growth since 1929 is greater, namely from 6½ per cent to 9 per cent. But I do not think that on the basis of these figures, anyone can hope or fear, as the case may be, that the United States is creeping into socialism.

III. The third item of my list concerns government interventions to alter the balance of economic power or to redistribute income and wealth. I can be very brief here. I do not see on the national agenda any serious proposal to alter in favor of labor organizations the balance of industrial power resulting from federal legislation in the 'thirties and 'forties and from the evolution of collective bargaining institutions. Certainly none is on the agenda of this Democratic Administration, although it is widely regarded as politically obligated to organized labor. The pendulum is swinging the other way, if at all. Organized labor represents an ever smaller proportion of the labor force. And for many of the practices and demands to which business objects, labor is on the defensive—politically, economically, and in public opinion. I do not expect businessmen to be satisfied with the balance of power that now exists, any more than union leaders are. But if the situation is unsatisfactory in either direction, it is surely unreasonable to blame the New Frontier for conditions that have prevailed for many years of both Democratic and Republican governments.

Redistribution of income and wealth by taxation and government transfer payments was in days gone by another rallying point for liberal political movements. The fire has gone out of this one too. The current liberal political movement, the New Frontier, is providing incentives for business investment through new tax legislation and new depreciation guidelines. The Kennedy Administration is, from all indications, about to be the vehicle for a general reduction in corporate and personal income tax rates, and in particular for substantial lowering of top-bracket rates.

It is true that the Administration has also tried to close certain tax loopholes and that it is pledged to further reforms of this nature. The joint effect of its proposals is not intended to be any significant shift either way in the relative tax burdens of rich and poor, but rather two other kinds of shifts—one to achieve more even-handed treatment of taxpayers in similar circumstances, and the other to provide relatively greater incentives for investment, growth, risk-taking, and efficiency and relatively smaller incentives for inefficient, wasteful, and consumptive activities. If I am not mistaken, these are the objectives that business advocates of tax reform have long espoused. But their reactions to tax proposals during the early '60s, quite frankly, are not easily reconciled with their expressed interest in these overall social and economic objectives. I refer—with the bias that may be expected from an ex-official of the Administration—to the lukewarm reception given the Administration's investment-incentive proposals, on the one hand, and, on the other, to the unmitigated hostility evoked by its proposals to withhold tax on dividend and interest income and to tighten the rules for expense account deductions.

IV. I come finally to the magnitude of public uses of economic resources. How much of the Gross National Product—whether it originates in private or governmental productive activity—is purchased by governments for public use? Is this public share growing too fast?

First let us gain the perspective a few figures may provide. In 1961, all governments together took 20½ per cent of the Gross National Product—federal defense uses, 9½ per cent; federal civilian uses, 1½ per cent; state and local governments, 9½ per cent. In 1929, all governments together took 9 per cent of GNP—the federal government 1½ per cent and state and local governments 7½ per cent. These figures exaggerate the real growth of the government share, for two reasons. The costs of government purchases, which are highly labor-intensive, have risen relative to other components of GNP. And, as I remarked before, 1961 was a poor cyclical year compared to 1929. If we correct for the gap in 1961 due to underemployment of resources and if we value all purchases of GNP at 1954 prices, we find the following: The total government share has risen from 10 per cent in 1929 to 18 per cent in 1961. The federal share rose from 1½ to 9½ per cent, while the state and local share remained constant at 8½ per cent. Virtually the entire increase in the government share is attributable to national defense.

I must explain, parenthetically, that government budgets as a whole have grown more rapidly than government purchases of goods and services. This is because these budgets include other types of transactions, loans, and transfer payments, which do not involve claims on productive resources. They do, nevertheless, require financing by taxes or other government receipts. For various reasons—partly the introduction of Social Security, partly the veterans' benefits and debt interest charges which are the legacy of the war—these transactions have risen faster since 1929 than purchases of goods and services, especially at the federal level. They undoubtedly bulk larger in the national economy than they did in 1929. It is not possible to find an appropriate national aggregate with which to compare these "non-purchase" transactions. GNP is not the appropriate concept, because it does not measure private "non-purchase" transactions either, and these, like government "non-purchases," have certainly grown faster than purchases of goods and services. For that reason, the comparison I am about to give, using GNP, overstates the relative growth of government. Total government receipts were 11 per cent of GNP in 1929 and 27 per cent in 1961. If we omit the receipts corresponding to defense expenditures and correct as before for underutilization in 1961, the 1961 figure is reduced to 16 per cent. And of these 16 percentage points, 4 are attributable to federal trust fund operations, mainly the Social Security funds. As I previously noted, the nation did assign to government in 1935 important new functions in social insurance. Nevertheless, and in spite of the handicap of inflation, total benefits paid by private life insurance companies have outpaced GNP since 1929, and other private health insurance and retirement plans have mushroomed.

In any case, civilian government is *not* preempting relatively more of the nation's productive potential than it was in 1929. And 1929, I remind you, was not only before the New Deal but a time when the population was growing less rapidly and the pressures for public services in education, transportation, recreation, and health were much less acute than now. The record does not justify fears that the growth of government threatens to leave no resources for private use. It may justify, on the contrary, fears that the burden of national defense has fallen too heavily on civilian government and relatively too lightly on private consumption.

But that is a matter on which opinions and tastes will and should differ. The proper level of government purchases cannot be decided in the market by individual decisions to buy or not to buy. The consumer is nonetheless sovereign, but his sovereignty must be exercised through the political process. You and I can differ in our consumption of breakfast foods to suit our tastes; but in the nature of the case we cannot consume different amounts of national defense. The role of the market is not an issue, since public services are intrinsically incapable of being allocated by the market. I remind you again that I am now talking about the uses of output, not the origins of output. The government can and does use the market to procure from private enterprise a large part of the goods and services it needs, rather than producing them for itself.

As to the inevitable differences of opinion concerning the proper level of public expenditures, my only stricture is this. Let us debate these differences in terms of relative national priorities for competing uses of resources—in terms of specific programs like education, space exploration, road-building, hospitals, trying to evaluate their importance at the margin both against one another and against household consumption and business investment. Let us not assume either, on the one side, that public uses of resources are per se wasteful and burdensome, or, on the other, that private uses reflecting consumer choices are per se frivolous and valueless. Let us not assume that because the regrettable burden of defense is necessarily a federal responsibility, other federal or governmental programs are obviously the marginal uses that must be curtailed whenever a turn of the Cold War pushes up the defense budget.

Right now, to be sure, the persistence of idle manpower and industrial capacity gives an air of unreality to these remarks about priorities. Those unused resources clearly indicate that government claims for resources have not been standing in the way of expansion of the private economy in the last few years; nor have private demands been so urgent as to leave no resources for expansion of public programs. Last spring a distinguished private financier wrote in a public letter to the President that it was a matter of grave concern to him and to the business community that private business investment had increased by only $1 billion over 1956, while government expenditures had increased by $43 billion. The weakness of private investment is indeed a matter of grave concern, and I mentioned above some of the efforts of the Administration to stimulate investment. But Mr. Rockefeller was implying that if government expenditure had grown less, private investment could have grown more. Actually the opposite is the case—had government expenditures grown less, private investment would have been even weaker; and had government expenditures grown more, private investment would have been *stronger*. For, during this period, private investment was not held down by any shortage of real productive resources or any lack of saving. It was held down by lack of final demand. And, I suspect, all business forecasters count an *in*crease, not a *de*crease, in government expenditures as a plus or bullish factor in projecting demand. The day may come again, I hope soon, when business and government are competing for the full-employment saving of the economy. But unfortunately that is not yet the case.

I know quite well, of course, that a fiscal stimulus to the economy can be given by tax reduction as well as by increased expenditure. In fact, I believe that we should in general set government expenditures at levels consonant with national priorities in the use of full-employment output, and that we should then set taxes at levels which induce enough private spending to employ fully all the resources not purchased by government. What does not make sense to me is to argue, as do so many business spokesmen these days, as follows: The economy needs the stimulus of a tax cut. But we can't afford a tax cut unless government expenditures are cut too. Therefore, to give the economy a stimulus, government expenditures must be cut. This is surely not the kind of economics on which business relies for forecasts. Why do businessmen revert to such a different brand of economic reasoning whenever public policy is up for discussion?

That is a digression from my main thesis. There certainly are real issues to be debated with respect to the share of government in the uses of national output. They are mainly concrete issues of national needs and priorities. They are not issues of social organization or of political philosophy, and it confuses and obscures them to try to frame them in those terms.

So far as domestic political economy is concerned, America does not stand at any crossroads. It is not faced with any grand choice between "isms." It is not beset by any war of economic classes, or threatened by any revolutionary expansion of the role of government. To the question "Is the Kennedy Administration anti-business?" the best answer is one that an academic colleague of mine used in another connection—I disagree with the question. The second-best answer is "No."

America certainly does face some very real economic problems —full employment, accelerated long-run growth, adaptation to technological change, provision for the expanding needs of a growing population. These will not be met by ideological slogans from the past. I hope businessmen will mobilize their experience and wisdom to help the nation and its government meet them.

Chapter 3

Barry's Economic Crusade

Barry Goldwater's campaign has developed his economic proposals more explicitly than any other aspect of his program. At first glance his major proposals seem to offer as much "echo" as "choice." He too wants to cut taxes, help state and local governments, raise Social Security benefits, and end the draft. But all resemblance to Administration programs and plans is superficial. Goldwater's proposals add up to the radical revolution that, to the delight of his fanatical followers and the dismay of the rest of us, he has always advocated.

Not that his present positions are faithful in detail to his previous writings or to his record in the Senate. Thanks to the influence of University of Chicago economist Milton Friedman, Goldwater's economic ideas seem to have gained in coherence and sophistication. This is less evident in campaign oratory than in the candidate's careful responses to questions on economic policy in *Business Week* of September 26, 1964.

Three basic themes run consistently through the Goldwater–Friedman economic program. A simple summary of them will make clear how drastic a change the Republican candidate has proposed.

1. The federal government should confine itself to providing a favorable climate for private economic activity. It should not try to steer the economy toward any particular goals. Target rates of unemployment and economic growth are conspicuously missing from Goldwater's pronouncements. There is no indication that he regards the record of the economy since 1957 as

Originally published in *The New Republic* (October 24, 1964), pp. 13–16.

unsatisfactory in these respects. Even the standard conservative goal of price stability receives little emphasis.

In Goldwater's view, which mirrors Friedman's, the government should not try to fight the business cycle. Rather, once having adopted the right monetary and fiscal policies, it should —apart from minor adjustments in timing—hold to them steadily through thick and thin, recession and inflation. Goldwater ignores the Employment Act of 1946, which commits the federal government to an active policy of economic stabilization in the interests of "maximum production, employment, and purchasing power."

2. The federal government should be reduced in economic size. To keep federal expenditures from rising with the growth of population and national income, Goldwater would give away in advance all of the normal growth of federal revenues. A little more than half would go into his five-year income tax reduction plan, the rest into other tax concessions and eventually into reduction of federal debt. This fiscal program is calculated to force the federal government gradually to strip itself of functions other than national defense and foreign policy, leaving them to be picked up, if at all, by state and local governments.

3. Government regulation of business undermines both freedom and economic efficiency. In the absence of misguided regulation, competition can be counted on to limit private economic power and to turn the self-interest of each into the welfare of all.

A conservative crusade might be expected to begin with a ringing denunciation of deficit spending and a solemn pledge to balance the budget. Although noises of this kind appear in some of his speeches, Goldwater has not taken a traditional conservative line. He seems to be a less fanatical opponent of budget deficits than were General Eisenhower or former Secretary of the Treasury George Humphrey, a prominent Goldwater supporter before San Francisco. At the famous Republican Governors' Conference in the spring of 1964 Eisenhower advocated that the federal government be required to balance its budget receipts and expenditures over every two-year period.

Goldwater's *Business Week* statement accepts no such straitjacket. Like every businessman, he says, the government must expect its receipts to vary unpredictably. It is not efficient to adjust programs to such ups and downs. Moreover, Goldwater obviously wants to be free to inaugurate his five-year tax-cut plan before the budget is literally in balance.

It would be pleasant to welcome the conservative wing of the GOP to the growing consensus that year-by-year, or two-year-by-two-year, budget balance is an impossibly foolish goal of fiscal policy. But the new converts have not come all the way. Goldwater will put up with deficits when the economy is below par, and he sees some value in the "built-in stabilizers," the automatic reductions in tax collections and increases in unemployment benefits which accompany and moderate recessions. But he opposes deliberate variation of federal tax rates or expenditures to offset waves in private spending. He wants "steady and dependable" tax rates and expenditure programs, designed to balance the budget "when the economy is prosperous and prices are stable." Fiscal policy is not to be used to bring the economy and the budget to this happy state.

Goldwater's passive fiscal strategy deviates from the Employment Act and contrasts with the practice of every Administration since the war. Every one, including Eisenhower's, has to a greater or lesser degree tried to pursue active countercyclical fiscal policy.

Following the spirit of recommendations by the blue-ribbon private Commission on Money and Credit in 1961, President Kennedy proposed to Congress a series of measures to make federal tax rates and expenditures more flexible and effective anti-recession tools. Clearly Goldwater will have none of this. He fatalistically accepts fluctuations both in business activity and in the balance of the federal budget.

Economists will have no difficulty discerning here the hand of their redoubtable conservative colleague Professor Friedman. He is skeptical of the economic importance of fiscal measures and stresses monetary policy instead. For Friedman the key variable is the stock of money—currency and coin in circulation plus commercial bank deposits. This is the province of the Federal Reserve System. But Friedman has long since despaired of the possibility of smoothing out cycles by monetary management. Even the best central bankers, he fears, will aggravate rather than moderate cycles—like a short-sighted housewife who tries to regulate the heat in her home by too frequent and too large adjustments of the thermostat. Friedman favors, for the Federal Reserve as well as for the budget, a "fixed-throttle" policy—keep the stock of money growing in good times and bad, at a constant pace roughly equal to the long-run growth rate of the economy. Interestingly enough, candidate Goldwater explicitly disavows this central recommendation of adviser Friedman. Indeed he uses the opportunity to make his obeisance to the principle of "the independent Federal Reserve System," a traditional conservative ritual somehow omitted from the Republican platform.

This is not the only medicine in Dr. Friedman's kit that proved too strong. Another is the proposal to cut the dollar loose from gold, letting it fluctuate freely in value in the foreign exchange markets. In *Business Week* Goldwater says: "We should stand ready to honor our commitments and sell our gold without question." Nevertheless it is an interesting irony that, in contrast to the campaign of 1960, financial circles identify the Republican candidate less firmly than his opponent with the maintenance of the gold standard.

The most eye-catching of Goldwater's economic proposals, of course, is his pledge to reduce all federal income tax liabilities, corporate as well as individual, by 25 per cent. This reduction would occur in five equal yearly installments according to a fixed and automatic schedule. When the plan is to start is unclear. In speeches Goldwater promises that "one of my first actions in the White House" will be to ask Congress to enact it. In *Business Week* he finds it "impossible to name the precise date" the cuts can take effect, for this can occur "only when the upward trend in spending has been brought to a halt and deficits in good times have been eliminated."

Several features of the proposal deserve comment:

1. Under existing tax laws the normal growth of the economy increases federal revenues about 5 per cent, or $6 billion, a year. The Goldwater plan would give back to income-tax payers a little more than half this normal yearly increment, about $3½ billion. In addition, Goldwater favors reducing the "host of

nuisance taxes," and he also proposes credits against income taxes for local school taxes and for tuition, fees, and gifts paid to educational institutions. The Republican platform also promises tax credits to aged citizens for medical and hospital insurance. Revenue losses involved cannot be estimated without more precise specification of these schemes, but they are potentially enormous.

As in other instances, Goldwater's voice is an echo, though a distorted and exaggerated echo, of President Johnson's. The Kennedy–Johnson Administration has been worried about the "drag" on the economy created by the automatic growth of the federal tax take, when it is not matched by equivalent growth of government or business spending. This was one of the motivations for the recent tax cut, and it has led President Johnson and his chief economic adviser, Walter Heller, to contemplate publicly the need for future "fiscal dividends."

2. Characteristically the Goldwater proposal immobilizes federal fiscal policy. The scheduled tax cuts proceed inexorably whether the future brings inflation or recession, more international tension or less. Recently Arthur F. Burns, chairman of President Eisenhower's Council of Economic Advisers, publicly chided Walter Heller for his suggestion that another fiscal dividend of unspecified size might be due in another year or two. "No careful economist," Burns wrote to the *New York Times,* "would ever make such a statement." We can only infer by extrapolation Burns' opinion of Goldwater's proposal and of the economists who devised it.

3. The plan greatly reduces the progressivity of federal income taxation. The high-bracket taxpayer benefits by a much bigger percentage of his income, before or after taxes than his low-bracket neighbor. This is Goldwater's notion of "the fair principle of equal treatment for all." Under the Revenue Act of 1964, individual income tax rates run from 14 to 70 per cent, compared to 20 to 91 per cent previously. Five years of Goldwater reductions would narrow the span of rates to 10.5 to 52.5 per cent. Meanwhile the corporation rate, already down from 52 to 48 per cent, would be further reduced to 36 per cent. Presumably this

is only the beginning of the assault on progressive taxation. Goldwater views the 25 per cent cut in everybody's tax liabilities as only a rough approximation to the basic tax reform he favors.

The central objective of the proposed tax reductions is to reduce the size of the federal government. All increases of revenue are to be given away in advance. No longer will the bureaucracy have to "work overtime to dream up new spending schemes to spend and even overspend" growing federal revenues.

Big Government is the main target of conservative anger. To Goldwater and his followers, the sheer size of the current federal budget is a greater evil than its deficit. Listen to Goldwater in Montgomery, Alabama, September 16, 1964. The federal colossus is steadily increasing in size, scope, and power, "engulfing our precious resources," subjugating the people and their state and local governments. The "explosive growth in nondefense spending must stop. The spread of federal bureaucracy must be arrested—before it cannibalizes us all." Never has so much indignation been generated for so little cause.

What are the facts? How big is the federal government relative to the national economy? And why?

1. One measure is the share of the federal government in the productive activity of the nation. What proportion of Gross National Product originates in the federal government? This measure does not count federal purchases of products made by private business. It does count production of goods and services in the government or in government enterprises. Some of these, like TVA electricity, are sold to private customers. But most are personal services, rendered by military personnel or civil servants, at the same time produced in the government and used by the government.

In 1963 federal activity originated $29 billion of the $584 billion GNP. Of this, $17½ billion represented the military and civilian payrolls of the armed services. Federal activity apart from defense did not account for more than 2 per cent of GNP. In 1929 —before America's fall from innocence—the corresponding figure was 1 per cent. Some of this increase is illusory—government is a very labor-using activity and costs more relative to other goods and services than in 1929. Anyway if this is creeping socialism, the creep is pretty slow.

2. A second measure relates to federal purchases, rather than federal production, of goods and services. How much of the nation's output, wherever produced, does the federal government buy and use? How much does it leave for the use of private individuals, businesses, and state and local governments? In 1963 federal purchases (plus foreign-aid-financed exports) were $66 billion, of which $55 billion was for defense and space. Thus federal civilian programs (including foreign economic aid) consumed less than 2 per cent of GNP. The corresponding figure for 1929 is about 1 per cent. About half of the difference reflects simply the relative increase over the years in the cost of the things the government buys. It does not appear that federal civilian programs are "engulfing our precious resources."

3. There are federal expenditures other than purchases of goods and services, and it is quite true that these have risen dramatically. They amounted in 1963 to $49 billion, about 8½ per cent of GNP, while in 1929 they were only $1.3 billion, 1.3 per cent of GNP. These expenditures included in 1963: (a) $30 billion of "transfer" payments to individuals, for which no current productive services are rendered in return—Social Security benefits ($19 billion) and veterans' pensions and insurance benefits ($4½ billion) are the main examples; (b) interest on the federal debt ($7.7 billion net); (c) grants-in-aid to state and local governments ($9 billion); (d) agricultural subsidies ($3.3 billion).

Do these numbers imply a great federal encroachment into the domains of private citizens and state and local governments? It is impossible to give a quantitative answer. Gross National Product is not the proper reference for comparison. In these transactions the government is neither a producer and seller nor a purchaser and consumer of goods and services. These expenditures do not diminish the economic resources available to the rest of the economy. They do transfer command over resources—from Social Security taxpayers to Social Security beneficiaries, from general taxpayers to state and local governments, veterans, federal bondholders, etc. There are similar private transfers—gifts, pensions, insurance payments. Some of these—in particular private health insurance and retirement plans—have grown explosively since the war. But there is no overall total with which to compare the federal figure.

Anyway Barry Goldwater neither would nor could do much to shrink these expenditures or to retard their growth. Earlier noises to the contrary notwithstanding, he now favors the Social Security system and wants to increase old-age and survivors' benefits. He cannot escape interest on the federal debt or contractual obligations to veterans.

As for grants to state and local governments, Goldwater does not promise or threaten to reduce them. Instead he would replace the present system of grants-in-aid of specific objectives—highways, public assistance, housing, urban renewal, hospitals, education, etc.—with unconditional grants. He would allocate these among states mainly in proportion to federal income tax collections, but there would be supplements for low-income states and cities.

In a sense this is another "Me-too" proposal. The Administration was already known to be studying the idea of unconditional grants. But there are no doubt important differences. A Johnson program, we may hope, would supplement rather than scrap programmatic grants-in-aid and would gear total aid more to population and need than to tax collections. After all, the main reason for financing state and local governments with *federal* taxes is that many people, many problems, and many objectives cross state boundaries. We are a nation. Connecticut citizens do have an interest in the quality of rivers in Massachusetts, of highways in Wyoming, schools in Mississippi, and life in Harlem. We cannot leave it wholly up to fifty state legislatures to determine whether and how national resources are used to meet national needs.

In agriculture, Goldwater wants to liberate the farmer from government controls and subsidies and create a free market. Bravo! Most economists, whatever their political persuasion, share this objective. And, as Goldwater can confirm by asking his friend Ezra Taft Benson, most farm state politicians are just as unanimous and nonpartisan in rejecting it. Anyway Goldwater recognizes that farmers will have to be helped through the transition. So this policy could not save money very soon.

In short, the enormous and growing size of the federal government is a phony issue. Goldwater won't touch the amounts spent for national defense, interest on the debt, veterans' payments, Social Security, and grants to state and local governments. Leave these out and the colossus shrinks to about $20 billion in total expenditures. Within this total we may be sure that Goldwater's axe will fall not on irrigation projects for the Southwest but on those politically vulnerable federal programs—e.g. foreign economic aid, the Peace Corps, the anti-poverty package, the support of sciences and the arts, national parks, forests, and lands—which attest, however feebly, that America is still capable of compassion, foresight, and taste.

The conservative crusaders march against the power of the alien government, not just its size. The refrain is that ever-increasing federal regulation has hamstrung and crippled our free private enterprise system. How this mighty engine of progress continues to function at all, hobbled as it has been for so long by bureaucratic controls, is a real mystery. In any case Goldwater leads in his war of liberation a whole host of business and professional men and women, the impoverished and enslaved victims of regimentation.

But Goldwater's indictment of federal regulatory agencies in *Business Week* might surprise his supporters as well as his opponents. His complaint is that these agencies too assiduously defend the very interests they are supposed to be regulating, to the detriment of consumers and potential competitors. With this indictment most liberals and most economists would agree. But the remedy is not just wholesale scrapping of regulation. In some cases, less regulation would indeed mean more competition, with benefit to the consuming public. This was the gist of President Kennedy's message to the Congress on transportation. In other cases, continued but reoriented regulation is essential, either to maintain effective competition or to protect and inform consumers when competition cannot do so. Goldwater and his economists would do well to face some specific questions. For example: Was the government wrong and tyrannical to keep thalidomide off

the market? Does it advance the cause of freedom when installment lenders deceive the public about interest rates? Does the
government have no right to limit the commercial use of the
publicly owned channels it has licensed rent-free to private
broadcasters?

Denouncing the Administration's moral guideposts for wage
and price decisions, Goldwater tells the workingman and businessman to get the best wage or price he can. Once in the White
House, Goldwater would almost certainly regret his invitation to
unions and managements to let no larger considerations adulterate
their pursuit of self-interest. Anyway the invitation makes sense
only if, as Goldwater and his advisers evidently believe, competition so effectively polices the abuse of economic power that no
Presidential guideposts are necessary.

Goldwater's professed faith that free competition is the natural
state of the economy is either very naïve or very disingenuous.
Modern large-scale technology limits the number of viable firms
in many industries, and the rivals do not have to conspire explicitly in order to understand their joint interest in avoiding
price-cutting and other forms of aggressive competition. Competition is not an indigenous plant. It has to be carefully cultivated
and constantly protected. Goldwater favors "vigorous and fair
antitrust enforcement," to keep markets "as competitive as possible" but not to be "used simply to attack bigness." That is
nowhere near tough enough. Logically the first and strongest
plank in Barry Goldwater's economic platform should commit
him to a much more far-reaching antitrust and anti-bigness policy
than we have ever had. In its absence, the high-principled crusade
for freedom looks very much like a crusade of well-heeled
Poujadistes out for more money and less taxes.

Chapter 4

The New Era of Good Feeling Between
Business and Government

During the past two years a quiet revolution has been occurring in United States economic policy and, what is even more important for the longer run, in the terms and the tone of public discussion of the role of the government in the economy. The federal government has accepted, more explicitly and completely than before, responsibility for the overall performance of the economy. The hard and bitter ideological lines that for decades dominated the national debate on the federal government's economic role are rapidly dissolving. They are being replaced by an "era of good feeling," in which there will, to be sure, be disagreements about policies, but ones that can be argued in much less doctrinaire and more pragmatic terms. This development is a considerable victory for the economist, who has long been frustrated in this country by the proclivity of practical men of affairs to place doctrinaire aphorisms above the findings of economic science.

To provide some background for these developments, I must go back to the 1930s. The New Deal, of course, worked a remarkable transformation of the relationship of the federal government to the economy. The government assumed responsibilities and powers in many fields—social insurance, unemployment relief, labor relations, securities markets, resource development, housing, etc.—that in the '20s had been left to private business or to state and local governments. At first, frightened by the complete collapse in 1932 and 1933 and its possible political dangers, members of the business and financial community supported, or

Originally published in *Challenge* (June 1965), pp. 23–26.

at least acquiesced in, Roosevelt's program. But as soon as they had been saved, they turned bitterly on their rescuers. For almost thirty years, with time out only for the Second World War, they fought the New Deal. A whole ideology was built and relentlessly propagated to oppose "centralized government" in the name of economic individualism, freedom, and the American free enterprise system. It is one of the ironies of history that when in 1964 the true believers of this ideology—indeed in all its counter-revolutionary implications—succeeded in capturing a major political party, they were deserted by the business and financial leadership that had originally promoted the hard antigovernment line.

Most New Deal measures were specific pragmatic responses to social evils, injustices, and other problems that had become apparent in the Depression. The Roosevelt Administration was free of the ideological principles which immobilized Hoover, against his own humanitarian instincts, while the economy collapsed and people lost jobs and starved. But it did not really have any overall economic program for restoring full prosperity and full employment.

But meanwhile an intellectual revolution was occurring in economics—under the leadership of John Maynard Keynes in England and Alvin Hansen in the United States. The new doctrine focused on an aspect of government policy not very much emphasized by the New Deal, namely the budget. The idea is really quite simple: When there is too little spending on goods and services in the economy to employ all the labor force, the government should either spend more itself, or induce other people to spend more through such means as lowering their taxes or adding to their welfare payments. Thus the objective of fiscal policy is not to balance the budget but to balance the economy—that is, to assure that there is enough demand for all the production of which the economy is capable. The budget of a great central government should not be viewed in narrow Micawberesque terms appropriate, if to anyone, to a family or a small shopkeeper.

In the perspective of history this must be regarded as a conservative doctrine. For it put to rout the Marxists, who claimed that capitalism was doomed to depression and unemployment.

It showed how these evils could be remedied without any fundamental changes in the structure of society. Nevertheless, many conservative spokesmen for the business and financial interests in this country saw Keynesian economics as a threat and bitterly denounced it. They saw the balanced-budget principle as the last defense against enlargement of the sphere of government and against inflation. The Committee for Economic Development, formed at the end of the war, took a much saner attitude, but its influence seemed to wane during the 1950s.

Roosevelt never really adopted an all-out Keynesian attack on the Depression until defense preparations in 1940 and 1941 forced him to do so for other reasons (and with the beneficent results in terms of higher employment and production that Keynesian economics had predicted). In 1932 Roosevelt had criticized Hoover for failing to balance the budget. Of course Roosevelt could not balance it either, especially if he was going to do anything for the country. Keynes' ideas occasionally came in handy to excuse this failure, but it can scarcely be said that the New Deal was really Keynesian.

During the war, however, Keynesian ideas caught on throughout the Western world. The contrast of full employment and high production in wartime with the unemployment and waste of the '30s, the fear that a collapse in demand with demobilization would create once again mass unemployment and depression, the feeling that the sacrifices of the war would not be worthwhile if this were allowed to happen—all this led to a resolution that governments must be responsible for managing the economy to assure the maintenance of prosperity and full employment. Throughout Western Europe this commitment and this governmental responsibility were accepted by all political parties and by all segments of the private economy. For example, in Britain, Conservatives no less than Laborites were committed to the management of government finances in the interest of full employment. This is no less true in Scandinavia, the Low Countries, France, and even in Germany, where "free enterprise" ideas have supposedly found a haven. In all these countries political parties may differ, and business and labor disagree, about such matters as nationalization of industry, the burdens of taxation, and the regulation of prices and wages, but they all take it for granted that the government's budgetary and monetary powers must be used to manage total demand and to maintain full employment and steady economic growth.

The same sentiments were strong in the United States in 1945–46, and they led to passage of the Employment Act of 1946. This Act, passed by large bipartisan majorities, states that it is the policy of the U.S. to use all the powers of the federal government to maintain "maximum employment, production, and purchasing power." To this end, the President was charged to report to the Congress at least once a year on how well the economy was doing and what the government was doing to improve its performance. To help him carry out this responsibility, he was given the Council of Economic Advisers.

The Employment Act, in which the Government acknowledged both its power and responsibility for "affording job opportunities for all those willing and able to work" symbolized the great change wrought by the Depression in America's conscience and understanding with respect to unemployment. Only 15 years before, the predominant opinion was that unemployment was the fault of the unemployed and that the government neither could nor should do anything about it.

But subsequent developments in the U.S. were quite different from those in Western Europe. The American business and financial establishment, unlike its European counterparts, was in no mood to accept the new role of government in the economy in either of its aspects—the structural reforms of the New Deal or the Keynesian management of total demand envisaged in the Employment Act. Its determination was hardened by the evident ambition of the Truman Administration to advance further toward the "welfare state." In any event, the business and financial community adopted an antigovernment stance that dominated American politics and, in my opinion, crippled American economic policy until very recently. With respect to fiscal policy, balancing the budget and keeping it small became the touchstones of responsibility and respectability. There was strong opposition to deliberate use of the budget to stabilize demand and employment at high levels.

The Administration of President Eisenhower accentuated this trend in orthodox opinion. The President himself was a very strong advocate of "fiscal responsibility," increasingly so as his term went on. Repeatedly he spoke about budget deficits, federal debt, and high government expenditures in terms of simple home-spun morality. He was supported and encouraged in this stand by his Secretary of the Treasury, George Humphrey. Emphasis on sound finance did not exempt the Eisenhower Administration from deficits, unexpected though they may have been. In the fiscal year 1959, the budget wound up $12½ billion in the red—the recession of 1958 cut sharply the taxable incomes of individuals and corporations. Eisenhower economized in his next budget, so as to go out of office with the books in balance. There seems little doubt that this attempt was poorly timed and contributed to the recession of 1960.

"Fiscal responsibility" was one of the few outlets available to the conservatives who came to power in the Eisenhower years. It did not prove possible or politically wise to dismantle the New Deal and all its works.

Antigovernment sentiment reached a fever pitch in 1961 and 1962. The business and financial communities were very suspicious of the Kennedy Administration. Before he had a chance to take office, Kennedy was cast in the familiar enemy role previously occupied by Truman and Roosevelt. Nothing Kennedy could do or say made any difference. It had been decided he was "anti-business." Actually, Kennedy—conscious of his thin-edge popular majority, aware of the conservatism of both parties in his Congress, convinced that he needed a united country behind him for international reasons—leaned over backward to try to gain the confidence and cooperation of business and finance. One example: Business received from the Kennedy Administration—though it offered no gratitude in return—what the Eisenhower Administration had never given: accelerated depreciation of capital assets for tax purposes.

So far as the Employment Act was concerned, this climate of opinion put fiscal policy under wraps. Balance was the official proclaimed objective of the first two Kennedy budgets, even though the economy obviously needed an expansion of demand

and of employment. Fiscal policy was more expansionary in deed than in word, because increased expenditures for the defense and space efforts were regarded as legitimate reasons for departing from "sound" budget plans.

The one famous and dramatic instance in which Kennedy did speak and act against business was the battle over steel prices in April 1962. This—and the heat of his initial anger at what he regarded as a double cross by the industry—gave to those who were hungry for proof anyway the clinching demonstration that he was "anti-business."

In June 1962 at Yale, Kennedy gave voice to his weariness with ideological battle cries and labels. He said, essentially, that the important problems of government were technical and complex, to be solved by open-minded pragmatic reason rather than by slogans, myths, and the doctrinaire application of simple principles. He appealed to the business community to stop its obsessive worry whether this or that policy or official is "anti-business" or not. This speech itself was, however, regarded as new confirmation that Kennedy was anti-business.

At about the same time Kennedy was persuaded of the futility of seeking a balanced budget, which was gaining him neither economic expansion nor political points. He therefore decided to recommend a major tax cut. But conservative opposition inside and outside the Congress was strong enough to delay enactment until the spring of 1964.

I believe the atmosphere was improving in 1963 even before Lyndon Johnson became President. Some of the fruits of the Administration's pro-business measures, like accelerated depreciation, were becoming apparent to their beneficiaries. The tax cut itself had considerable appeal, and it was neutrally distributed among taxpayers. Many business and financial leaders were probably ready to climb down from the limb where they were perched out of suspicion of Kennedy. The change of presidency gave them the opportunity to do so without losing face.

Then Goldwater was nominated. His caricature of an anti-government, antifederal ideology undoubtedly drove businessmen into Johnson's camp—not simply on election day but in the sense that they grew more willing to accept government's role in the economy and consider government actions on their case-by-case merits.

The tax cut worked. More important for the long run, it was perceived to work. It kept the business expansion going, reduced unemployment, raised corporate profits—and all without the slightest signs of inflation. Success talks, and this one has solidified support for the continuous management of demand, through the budget, contemplated so long ago by the Employment Act and practiced long since in every European country. In 1965—more precisely the second half of 1965—the Administration figures the economy will need another stimulus. This will be administered largely via cuts in excise taxes and improvements in Social Security benefits. We can expect it to be routine in the future for the Administration to propose a fiscal program designed to close any gap between "maximum" and actually expected levels of "employment, production, and purchasing power." Moreover, the President has proposed, as Kennedy did in 1962, three other standby measures to prevent and eliminate such gaps. One is quick enactment of a temporary prepackaged tax cut. Another is permanent improvement of unemployment insurance so that benefits increase automatically when the incidence of unemployment is high. A third is a shelf of public works.

In the future there will certainly be controversy over *how* the Administration is managing the economy. But there will be much less basic and diversionary controversy over *whether* the government should be in this business at all. Talk of deficits and public debt will no longer be decisive; budgets will be formulated and criticized for their economic consequences.

The same relaxation of ideological tensions extends to the details of the program to build the Great Society. These are judged and discussed much less in terms of rigid principles about what is and is not proper for the government to do, and much more in terms of their specific effects and effectiveness. The idea that we have a mixed economy is widely accepted—soon even the AMA will get the word.

There are two other factors that contribute to the climate of good feeling and national consensus in which the Great Society program is being launched. One is the détente in the Cold War, combined with the completion of the defense buildup engineered by President Kennedy. This means that defense expenditures will very likely remain stationary or decline. Consequently new civilian programs can be undertaken without making the federal budget grow to sizes that frighten conservative opinion. The normal growth of national product is $30–35 billions a year, and of this $6–7 billions will flow into the Federal Treasury in added revenue each year without any change in tax rates whatever. This means that Great Society programs can be financed relatively painlessly so long as the economy is kept on an upward growth track. Indeed we can have all this and the heaven of occasional tax reduction too. Of course, all bets on this score will be off if events in Southeast Asia develop into another Korea, requiring massive increases in military expenditures.

The second factor is related to the one just discussed. It is a point that Walter Lippmann has correctly stressed: The Great Society is not a redistributive program. President Johnson does not raise the question of distributive justice, as between rich and poor or capital and labor. He does not propose a different Deal of the same cards, whether Square or New or Fair. He proposes to solve the pressing problems of the society—poverty, education, health, etc.—out of the vast annual increment in national product and without enlarging the government's share of national product. This emphasis on an ever-growing pie, rather than on slicing up a given pie in a new way, is well designed, I think, to attract widespread support, or at least consent, to his program.

PART II

FISCAL POLICY, THE BUDGET, AND GROWTH

Introduction

Some of the issues raised in passing in Part I concern the balance and size of the federal budget. These are treated more fully in the essays of Part II. Four basic points are made. First, budget expenditures and taxes are powerful tools of economic stabilization and should be deliberately used for this purpose. Second, the size of the budget should reflect a rational calculation of national priorities. It is not true that the only good budget is a small budget. National resources should be allocated between public and private uses so that the last dollar spent in each use is of the same social utility. Third, there is no intrinsic need or virtue in balancing the federal budget or limiting the federal debt. These objectives may be politically important, but they are wholly irrelevant to the economic principles of fiscal policy. Fourth, it may be economically desirable under full employment conditions for the government to augment private saving by running a surplus. Channeling government saving into private investment, with the help of an easy monetary policy and tax incentives, could accelerate economic growth.

Chapter 5 is an attack on the balanced-budget fetish. It attempts to show why the Puritan maxim that it is prudent to spend less than one's receipts cannot be applied to everybody in the economy. One man's surplus is inevitably another man's or a government's deficit. In particular, the essay argues, the maxim is inapplicable to the federal government.

An earlier essay taking issue with the Eisenhower Administration's preoccupation to limit the size of the budget and the federal debt is reprinted as Chapter 6. I felt at the time that the prevailing financial orthodoxy was threatening even the defense of the country. In retrospect this fear appears exaggerated, for it seems that published reports at the time overestimated Soviet military strength. Nevertheless, I believe the point still holds that the Administration was placing too much emphasis on irrelevant financial objectives at the expense of the real needs of the country.

Chapter 7 was originally part of a symposium on the consequences for the United States of the end of the long era in which this continent was virtually invulnerable to foreign military attack. I consider here the charge, often made by left-wing foreign critics, that defense spending is essential to the American economy. To the contrary, I argue that defense is a real burden. I also touch on the international monetary implications of the passing of America's unique invulnerability, a subject to which I return in Part IV.

The fourth essay in this section is a rather extreme statement of the fourth point above, namely that a budget surplus can under full employment conditions augment the resources available for investment and growth. The other necessary component of such a policy is to provide enough investment incentives to make sure that demand is maintained at full employment levels, i.e. that the additional saving is actually invested in plant and equipment. Otherwise it will be wasted in unemployment and underproduction.

The article was poorly timed, for two reasons. First, the dominating problem at the time and ever since has been how to restore full employment rather than how to promote more saving. Second, U.S. balance-of-payments difficulties have in practice ruled out the aggressive use of monetary policy to promote domestic investment and growth. Indeed the economy has been pushed away from the "tight budget–easy money" mix advocated in Chapter 8 to an "easy budget–tight money" mix to try to solve simultaneously the unemployment and balance-of-payments problems. Furthermore, subsequent research by a number of economists on the relation of investment and growth indicates that the essay probably overstates the additional growth that more investment could yield. Nevertheless I reprint the article in its original form, as indicative of the way in which various tools of government policy can be combined to pursue simultaneously the goals of full employment and accelerated growth. Future circumstances may be more favorable to the "tight budget–easy money" mixture I advocated. I still think an increase in the economy's ratio of investment to full employment Gross National Product would be desirable. Incidentally, recent reductions in defense requirements, relative to GNP, mean that a growth policy need not be so hard on consumption as Chapter 8 indicates.

The final essay of this Part is a later and more technical presentation of the rationale for government policy to promote economic growth. The paper argues that in the absence of a growth policy, society is likely to make insufficient provision for the future.

Chapter 5

Deficit, Deficit, Who's Got the Deficit?

For every buyer there must be a seller, and for every lender a borrower. One man's expenditure is another's receipt. My debts are your assets, my deficit your surplus.

If each of us was consistently "neither borrower nor lender," as Polonius advised, no one would ever need to violate the revered wisdom of Mr. Micawber. But if the prudent among us insist on running and lending surpluses, some of the rest of us are willy-nilly going to borrow to finance budget deficits.

In the United States today one budget that is usually left holding a deficit is that of the federal government. When no one else borrows the surpluses of the thrifty, the Treasury ends up doing so. Since the role of debtor and borrower is thought to be particularly unbecoming to the federal government, the nation feels frustrated and guilty.

Unhappily, crucial decisions of economic policy too often reflect blind reactions to these feelings. The truisms that borrowing is the counterpart of lending and deficits the counterpart of surpluses are overlooked in popular and Congressional discussions of government budgets and taxes. Both guilt feelings and policy are based on serious misunderstanding of the origins of federal budget deficits and surpluses.

American *households* and *financial institutions* consistently run financial surpluses. They have money to lend, beyond their own needs to borrow. Figure 5.1 shows the growth in their combined surpluses since the war; it also shows some tendency for

Originally published in *The New Republic* (January 19, 1963), pp. 10–12.

Figure 5.1. Financial Surpluses of Consumers, Nonprofit Institutions, and Financial Institutions, 1947–61.

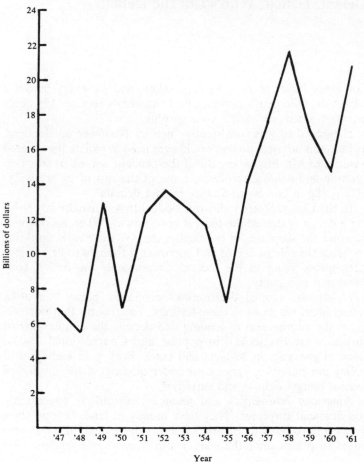

Source: Board of Governors of the Federal Reserve System

these surpluses to rise in periods of recession and slack business activity. Of course, many private households have financial deficits. They pay out more than their incomes for food, clothing, cars, appliances, houses, taxes, and so on. They draw on savings accounts, redeem savings bonds, sell securities, mortgage houses, or incur installment debt. But deficit households are far outweighed by surplus households. As a group American *households* and *non-profit institutions* have in recent years shown a net financial surplus averaging about $15 billion a year—that is, households are ready to lend, or to put into equity investments, about $15 billion a year more than they are prepared to borrow. In addition, *financial institutions* regularly generate a lendable surplus, now of the order of $5 billion a year. For the most part these institutions—banks, savings and loan associations, insurance companies, pension funds, and the like—are simply intermediaries which borrow and relend the public's money. Their surpluses result from the fact that they earn more from their lending operations than they distribute or credit to their depositors, shareowners, and policyholders.

Who is to use the $20 billion of surplus funds available from households and financial institutions? *State and local governments* as a group have been averaging $3–4 billion a year of net borrowing. Pressures of the expanding populations of children, adults, houses, and automobiles, plus the difficulties of increasing tax revenues, force these governments to borrow in spite of strictures against government debt. *Unincorporated businesses,* including farms, absorb another $3–4 billion. To the rest of the world we can lend perhaps $2 billion a year. We cannot lend abroad—net—more than the surplus of our exports over our imports of goods and services, and some of that surplus we give away in foreign aid. We have to earn the lendable surplus in tough international competition. Recent experience shows clearly that when we try to lend and invest too much money abroad, we either have to borrow it back or else pay in gold.

These borrowers account for $8–10 billion. The remainder—some $10–12 billion—must be used either by *nonfinancial corporate business* or by the *federal government.* Only if corporations as a group take $10–12 billion of external funds, by borrowing or issuing new equities, can the federal government expect to break even. This is, moreover, an understatement of what is required to keep the federal debt from rising, for the federal government itself provides annually $3 to $4 billion of new lending; the Treasury would have to borrow to finance these federal lending programs even if the government absorbed no *net* funds from the economy. It is *gross* federal borrowing that offends the conservative fiscal conscience, whether or not the proceeds are used to acquire other financial assets.

The moral is inescapable, if startling. If you would like the federal deficit to be smaller, the deficits of business must be bigger. Would you like the federal government to run a surplus and reduce its debt? Then business deficits must be big enough to absorb that surplus as well as the funds available from households and financial institutions.

That does not mean that business must run at a loss—quite the contrary. Sometimes, it is true, unprofitable businesses are forced to borrow or to spend financial reserves just to stay afloat; this was a major reason for business deficits in the depths of the Great Depression. But normally it is businesses with good profits and good prospects that borrow or sell new shares of stock, in order to finance expansion and modernization. As the President of American Telephone and Telegraph can testify, heavy reliance on outside funds, far from being a distress symptom, is an index and instrument of growth in the profitability and worth of the corporation. The incurring of financial deficits by business firms —or by households and governments for that matter—does not usually mean that such institutions are living beyond their means and consuming their capital. Financial deficits are typically the means of accumulating nonfinancial assets—real property in the form of inventories, buildings, and equipment.

When does business run big deficits? When do corporations draw heavily on the capital markets? The record is clear: when business is very good, when sales are pressing hard on capacity, when businessmen see further expansion ahead. Though corporations' internal funds—depreciation allowances and plowed-back profits—are large during boom times, their investment programs are even larger.

Figure 5.2. Net Financial Surpluses and Deficits of the Federal Government and of Nonfinancial Corporations, 1947–61

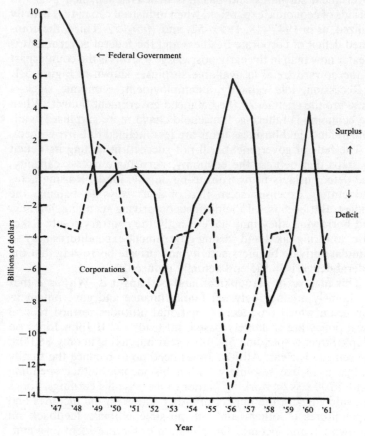

Source: Board of Governors of the Federal Reserve System

Figure 5.2 shows the financial deficits or surpluses of corporate business and of the federal government since the war. Three facts stand out. First, the federal government has big deficits when corporations run surpluses or small deficits and vice versa. Second, government surpluses and business deficits reach their peaks in periods of economic expansion, when industrial capacity is heavily utilized, as in 1947–48, 1951–52, and 1956–57. Third, the combined deficit of corporate business and the federal government is greater now than in the early postwar years; this is the counterpart of the upward trend in available surpluses shown in Figure 5.1.

Recession, idle capacity, unemployment, economic slack— these are the enemies of the balanced government budget. When the economy is faltering, households have more surpluses available to lend, and business firms are less inclined to borrow them.

The federal government will not succeed in cutting its deficit by steps that depress the economy, perpetuate excess capacity, and deter business firms from using outside funds. Raising taxes and cutting expenses seem like obvious ways to balance the budget. But because of their effects on private spending, lending, and borrowing, they may have exactly the contrary result. Likewise, lowering taxes and raising government expenditures may so stimulate private business activity and private borrowing that the federal deficit is in the end actually reduced.

This may seem paradoxical, and perhaps it is. Why is it that the homely analogy between family finance and government finance, on which our decisive national attitudes toward federal fiscal policy are so largely based, misleads us? If John Jones on Maple Street is spending $8,700 a year but taking in only $8,000, the remedy is clear. All Mr. Jones need do to balance the family budget is to live resolutely within his income, either spending some $700 less or working harder to increase his earnings. Jones can safely ignore the impact of either action on the incomes and expenditures of others and the possible ultimate feedback on his own job and income. The situation of the President on Pennsylvania Avenue, spending $87 billion a year against tax revenues of $80 billion is quite different. Suppose that he spends $7 billion less, or tries through higher tax rates to boost federal revenues by $7 billion. He cannot ignore the inevitable boomerang effect on federal finances. These measures will lower taxpayers' receipts, expenditures, and taxable incomes. The federal deficit will be reduced by much less than $7 billion; perhaps it will even be increased.

Incidentally, many of the very critics who are most vocal in chiding the government for fiscal sin advocate policies that would make fiscal virtue even more elusive. They want to keep private borrowing in check by the use of tight credit policies and high interest rates. They want to increase corporations' *internal* flow of funds by bigger depreciation allowances and higher profit margins, making business still less dependent on external funds to finance investment, even in boom times. When these apostles of sound finance also tell the government to shun external finance, have they done their arithmetic? If everyone is self-financing, who will borrow the surpluses?

The nation is paying a high price for the misapplied homely wisdom that guides federal fiscal policy. The real toll is measured by unemployment, idle capacity, lost production, and sluggish economic growth. But fiscal conservatism is also self-defeating. It does not even achieve its own aim, the avoidance of government deficits. Federal fiscal and monetary policies consciously and unashamedly designed to stimulate the economy would have sufficient justification in economic expansion itself. But they might well "improve" the federal budget too—by inducing business to use the private surpluses that now have no destination other than a rising federal debt.

Chapter 6

Defense, Dollars, and Doctrines

The force of ideas in history has never been better described than in the famous concluding passage of John Maynard Keynes' *General Theory of Employment, Interest, and Money:*

> The ideas of economists and political philosophers, both when they are right and when they are wrong, are more powerful than is commonly understood. Indeed the world is ruled by little else. Practical men, who believe themselves to be quite exempt from any intellectual influences, are usually the slaves of some defunct economist. Madmen in authority, who hear voices in the air, are distilling their frenzy from some academic scribbler of a few years back. I am sure that the power of vested interests is vastly exaggerated compared with the gradual encroachment of ideas. Not, indeed, immediately, but after a certain interval; for in the field of economic and political philosophy there are not many who are influenced by new theories after they are twenty-five or thirty years of age, so that the ideas which civil servants and politicians and even agitators apply to current events are not likely to be the newest. But, soon or late, it is ideas, not vested interests, which are dangerous for good or evil.

The recent economic policies of the United States government provide a dramatic confirmation of Keynes' high estimate of the power of economic ideology. In this instance the ideas have been dangerous for evil; the policies they have dictated have cost the United States its world leadership and gravely threatened its survival as a nation. The central doctrine of the economic

Originally published in *The Yale Review, 47* (March 1958), 321–34.

philosophy that has produced this disaster is very simple: Government intervention in economic life—spending, taxing, borrowing, regulating—is an evil to be minimized; man's needs are best accommodated, and progress is most rapid, when private enterprise flourishes unfettered by government regulations and unburdened by the dead weight of government activity. This economic philosophy has a long and honorable tradition, going back to Adam Smith (*Wealth of Nations,* 1776) and the classical economists of the nineteenth century. Throughout much of their history, classical economic ideas have been a power for good. As the intellectual basis for the liberation of economic life from feudal restrictions and from provincial and national barriers to trade, they assisted in the industrial transformation of the Western world in the past century and a half. At other times, however, the doctrine of minimal government has been singularly inappropriate. Twice in this century men of strong and sincere devotion to this orthodox economic position have been in power in Washington at times when the situation cried out for expansion rather than limitation of federal activity and initiative.

Once was the depression of 1929–32, when the stern principles and strong character of President Hoover shaped the economic policies of the federal government. Against common sense, against his own humanitarian instincts, against strong political pressures, Herbert Hoover refused to use the power and purse of the federal government to aid the victims of the Great Depression. His stubborn adherence to principle was in a way admirable; unhappily the doctrines that commanded his devotion were 100 per cent wrong for the situation he confronted. The nation slid to the brink of revolution, from which it was saved less by the fact that Roosevelt had in the beginning any different economic views than by the fact that Roosevelt was a flexible and pragmatic politician.

Orthodox fiscal doctrines have again dominated our policies during the five years since 1953, and again they have brought the nation to the brink of catastrophe, a different and infinitely more serious catastrophe than the internal collapse of 1932. We have had once again a businessman's administration, and once more it has been demonstrated that there is no one more doctrinaire and impractical in public affairs than some successful practical men of private affairs. This time it is not the President who has a firm and well-defined ideological position but the men on whom he has relied. The economic doctrines loyally held by former Secretary of the Treasury Humphrey, former Secretary of Defense Wilson, and Chairman Martin of the Federal Reserve have been the powerful determinants of the Administration's budgetary and monetary policies. In Congress leadership in both parties has passed to men of similar beliefs, such as Senators Johnson and Knowland. The climate of opinion since 1953 has given new power and prestige to the extreme antigovernment views of Senator Byrd.

No decision of our government is more important, in the 1950s, than the decision of how much of the vast productive resources of the nation to devote to the defense of the United States and of the free world. Defense must be broadly interpreted. In the short run, our security depends on the armaments we already have and the personnel we have to man them. In a longer view, it depends on our production of more armaments, and on our program of research and development of new weapons. In a still longer view, tomorrow's defense depends on today's support of basic science, including the education and recruitment of the ablest talent of the maturing generation. And both today and tomorrow, our security is inextricably wound up with the economic, social, and military health of our allies and with the progress of the uncommitted and underdeveloped nations of the world.

To all of these programs the federal budget is the key. It is no exaggeration to say that our defense policy, our foreign aid policy, and inevitably our entire foreign policy have been shaped by the men who have made our fiscal policy. Humphrey and Byrd have had more effect on our defense program and foreign policy than Dulles, or than Khrushchev.

A recent *New Yorker* cartoon showed a middle-aged middle-class wife commenting to her husband: "It's a great week for everybody. The Russians have the intercontinental ballistic missile, and we have the Edsel." The major economic and foreign policy of the Administration could not be more succinctly expressed. The response of the Administration to the news in August 1957 of Russia's success with missiles, which coincided with Russian diplomatic gains in Syria and the Arab world and with Russian intransigeance in disarmament negotiations, was a continuation of the vigorous effort of Secretary Wilson to *reduce* the rate of spending of the Defense Department by about $4 billion a year. At a time when the world situation cried out for accelerating and enlarging our defense effort, the Administration *released* money, labor, scientific talent, materials, and plant capacity. Since the ramifications of Pentagon decisions on contracts, subcontracts, orders, and jobs take time, the economic consequences of the Wilson cutbacks are still being felt. It will also take time to reverse them.

Leave aside the confusions and distractions created by the mysteries of public finance and focus on the simple and basic economic question: In what uses other than unemployment were these released resources to be absorbed? For what more pressing purposes were these resources released? For research and development of new consumer luxuries, for new plants in which to produce more consumers' goods, old and new, all to be marketed by the most advanced techniques of mass persuasion to a people who already enjoy the highest and most frivolous standard of living in history.

The policies of Secretaries Humphrey and Wilson in 1957 were not new. A reduction in the federal government's share of the national output has always been a prime goal of the Administration, and its ascendant position in Humphrey's scale of values showed in his ill-concealed frustration and anger that the 1958 budget was still so big. No sooner was Eisenhower installed in power than the Administration grasped with enthusiasm the proposition that nuclear weapons made it possible to have "more bang for a buck," more military power at less cost. The doctrine of "massive retaliation" was made as much in Treasury as in State. The United States turned its back on the concept of limited wars and on the maintenance of the costly manpower and conventional armaments necessary to be prepared to fight them. Taken seriously, the policy greatly reduces our freedom of action in case of local Communist aggression as in Korea. Lacking conventional arms, we can either precipitate a nuclear war with the Soviet Union or do nothing at all to oppose the aggression. The success of the policy as a deterrent depended on our maintaining a lead in nuclear weapons and the ability to deliver them. Now that lead has evaporated, perhaps been reversed. The same solicitude for the budget that has weakened us in conventional arms has enabled the Soviet Union to catch us and surpass us in the realm of nuclear weapons and rockets.

In the course of his two radio–TV addresses to the nation in defense of his budget in May 1957, the President said that the defense and foreign aid budgets could not be reduced without taking "reckless gambles" with the security of the free world. Thus he in effect admitted that these budgets were already too low. We are much too rich a country to keep our defenses at the margin of taking very serious risks to our very survival. A nation on the edge of starvation might of necessity be on the edge of insecurity. The United States has no private uses of resources so compelling that they justify keeping the Western world in such a precarious position that any reduction in the budget will gravely threaten security. We can afford more of a cushion than that, and we can't afford not to have it.

For the defense of North America against nuclear attack from the air, the government has done almost nothing. In May 1956 General Partridge, in command of continental air defense, testified before a Congressional committee that an adequate program— radar warning, interceptors, ground-to-air missiles, etc.—would cost $65 billion over the fifteen-year period 1951–65, and that scarcely any of this amount had yet been spent. Our civil defense program, as everyone knows, is a joke. The federal government has put no money into it, and it is not something that states, localities, and private individuals can do for themselves. Casualties could be greatly reduced by shelters, but we have not even made a beginning in building them. Similarly, industrial decentralization has been pursued only in a halfhearted way; we favor decentralization as long as it costs nothing. Meanwhile its greater geographical concentration makes American industry a more vulnerable target than its Soviet counterpart. Underground installation of certain vital industrial plants may be essential for the nation to survive an attack, but this is another area where we evidently have no program.

The catalogue of unfilled defense needs could be extended to requirements of a less immediate military nature but of equal or greater ultimate importance. Assistance in the economic development of Africa, Asia, and Latin America, and support of all levels of education in the United States itself would be high on an extended list. But enough examples have been given to make the essential point. The unfilled needs of defense are great and they are urgent. Whether we wish to try to meet them depends on how we weigh in the balance the urgency of these defense needs against the urgency of those private uses of resources that would have to be sacrificed. Anyone who appraises the luxury standard of living of the United States with the perspective of historical comparisons or comparisons with the rest of the contemporary world will strike the balance only one way. He will prefer to save our lives rather than our leisure; he will value freedom over fashion.

If reasonable men nevertheless oppose expansion of government defense programs, they must have loaded the other side of the scales with weighty considerations beyond the intrinsic importance of maintaining and increasing the consumption level of our population. What are the weighty considerations that tip the scales for men like Secretary Humphrey and Senator Byrd? They come from the classical economic philosophy of these men, and they may be summarized in three fears: (1) fear of the national debt, (2) fear of the long-run effects of large government budgets and high tax rates on the productivity of the economy, and (3) fear of inflation. Unfortunately for the suitability of the recent policies of the government but fortunately for the nation and the world, there is not enough substance to any of these fears, individually or in combination, to prevent us from doing what needs to be done to defend the free world.

1. The most pressing motivation for Secretary Wilson's heroic efforts at economy in the summer of 1957 was the $275 billion limit on the national debt, Senator Byrd's contribution to sound public finance. The Treasury feared that undiminished spending would pierce the $275 billion limit, at least temporarily until

tax receipts could roll in the following spring. The Administration preferred taking two or three 100,000-man whacks at the armed forces to facing the ire with which Senator Byrd and his orthodox friends of both parties in Congress would greet a request to raise the debt limit. Even in 1958 the Treasury asked only for a temporary $5 billion increase in the limit, and apologized for that. If the United States is destroyed, the history books, if any, can record their pride that the debt limit was never breached.

Imagine a rich country, with an annual national income over $400 billion a year, in debt to foreign countries to the tune of $275 billion, paying $8 billion a year interest to its external creditors. A debt of this size would be no calamity. The interest burden would be well within the nation's capacity to pay, and there would be no reason for the country to cripple itself in time of need by an arbitrary self-imposed debt limit. But at least there would be some real burden, and it would be prudent for those who manage the nation's economic affairs to give thought to its external debt. The United States has no such debt; indeed we are a net creditor of the rest of the world. Senator Byrd's ordinance of self-denial applies to an internal debt. The people of the United States are both debtor and creditor. The $8 billion a year in interest is not a diversion of our production to foreigners. It is paid by us as taxpayers to us as bondholders (either directly or to banks, insurance companies, pension funds, and other institutions that invest our savings in government bonds). Since the debt is, so to speak, within the family, its size can and should be the servant of public policy, not the master. Congress can in any case control the size of the debt by budgeting for surpluses or deficits as the occasion demands; the debt limit is quite superfluous, except for inhibiting the Treasury's ability to deal with seasonal variation in its disbursements and revenues. The debt limit represents a misdirected collective resolution to be good; its unchallenged appeal can only be based on semantic confusion. Under the debt limit, Uncle Sam fights with one hand tied behind his back, a handicap imposed neither by any necessity of nature nor any wile of his enemy, but by himself.

2. Americans take comfort in the enormous productive power of the country, still far in advance of the Soviet Union. One of

the orthodox arguments for minimal government is that the military strength of America and of the free world depends ultimately on this productive power and its continued growth. Twice the mobilization of America's productive power has saved the world, and if it is permitted to flourish and grow, this power will be our security once more. Our productive strength can be "sapped" and its growth arrested, we are told, by high government budgets, foreign aid, debt, taxation, and inflation. Then all will be lost.

This argument is wrong and dangerous, on several counts.

First, the revolution in the technology of destruction means that the next world war, if ever it comes, will be decided by forces in being, not by potential strength. The weapons that our factories *could* produce, our engineers *could* design, or our scientists *could* invent—could if they had plenty of time—will neither defend us nor retaliate. Even in the Second World War, the mobilization of our potential strength was almost too late. Hitler's economic base was much smaller than the Allies' potential, but his headstart almost won for him twice, once in the Battle of Britain and again in his last-minute rocket offensive. In a third world war, we may not have days, much less years.

Second, military strength is not achieved by making civilian goods. The way to become strong in producing aircraft is to produce aircraft and to build plants that produce aircraft. The way to have scientists and engineers skilled in missiles development is to develop missiles. Let us not fool ourselves that the use of talent and other resources to design, say, more automatic and more powerful automobiles is contributing to our national strength. Why was the United States the strongest power in the world in 1946? The plant capacity, the know-how, the technological lead that gave us our preeminent position (unimpaired, through our geographical good fortune, by any wartime devastation) were substantially the work of the war itself. If now the Soviet Union has overtaken us, it is not because their overall productive capacity exceeds ours—it still falls far short. But in the grim calculus of relative military strength, much of our vast production is just thrown away, while they have concentrated on building the capacity and advancing the technology of military strength.

Third, growth of our productive power requires expansion of government activities—federal, state, and local—as well as expansion of private activities. In the ideology of the Humphreys and the Byrds, dollars spent by governments are prima facie unproductive, dollars spent by private individuals and firms productive. In the eighteenth century the Physiocrats regarded only the tillers of land as productive; the remainder of society, no matter how busy, were viewed as unproductive parasites. Even Adam Smith reserved the adjective "productive" for makers of tangible goods, though he was willing to count artisans as well as farmers. Fortunately neither of these views was permitted to interfere with Western economic development. The derogation of the public servant (and of those whose pay is indirectly due to government) is a more recent and unhappily more serious version of the same fallacy. Government dollars spent for such things as fire and police protection, education, postal service, highways, parks, hospitals, libraries, sanitation, and flood control, need have no inferiority complex with respect to private dollars spent for steaks, television, freezers, alcohol, horse racing, gasoline, comic books, and golf. Classical economic ideology invests the processes by which private firms and households decide how much and on what to spend with rationality, sanctity, and purity. In contrast, the decision mechanisms of politics and bureaucracy are regarded as haphazard and often sordid. This contrast can be maintained only by an unduly cynical view of democratic political processes and an excessively idealized picture of the decision processes of consumers and businessmen. Do rational choices always come from consumers beset on every side by the cleverest stratagems of Madison Avenue? Can we be so sure of the wisdom of corporation managements contending with inadequate information about the future and with the conflicting pressures of their own constituent interest groups—stockholders, employees, customers, and creditors?

Finally, what of the gloomy prophecies that high rates of taxation will destroy the vitality of American capitalism by removing the incentives for effort and for risk-taking? While their public spokesmen have bombarded us with these predictions of calamity for twenty years or more, American businessmen have striven as earnestly and diligently as ever and the corporations they manage have engineered an unparalleled expansion of capital at risk in new plant and equipment. It is time to base economic policy on the evidence of history rather than on imaginary future catastrophes.

3. One justification of the bearish assessment of American capabilities that has dominated defense and budget policy is the fear that large budgets and high taxes would inhibit overall economic growth. In view of the overriding importance assigned to economic growth, it is ironic that the Administration has permitted our rate of growth to be retarded in the past two years in spite of, or perhaps because of, the restriction in government activity. This retardation is because of the third besetting fear that has shaped the economic policies of the Administration, the fear of inflation.

All good people dislike inflation, just as they oppose rainy weekends and traffic accidents. But, like many other evils, inflation is not an absolute and must be viewed in the perspective of competing evils. A society can suffer much worse maladies than inflation: for example, war, illiteracy, juvenile delinquency, racial disharmony, inadequate medical care. Our postwar inflation decade has also been a decade of unparalleled prosperity and improvement in standards of living.

Why is inflation in such bad repute? Most people make no distinction between moderate and gradual inflation (say 2–4 per cent per year) and certain notorious runaway inflations (100–1,000 per cent per year) like that in Germany after the First World War or in Japan after the Second World War. Though it is widely pontificated that the first variety invariably leads to the second, there is no evidence to support this view; and the postwar examples of the United States, Britain, and a number of other Western countries so far refute it. A common denominator of disastrous inflations is the occurrence of severe shocks to the entire political, economic, and social fabric of the society: devastation or defeat in war, revolution, reparations, or other heavy external obligations. Under the impact of such cataclysms the population loses confidence in the currency and in other government obligations. Obviously the circumstances that gradually push up the price level in the peacetime United States are of an entirely different order.

The other main reason for inflation's bad name is that lenders of all kinds—people with currency in the mattress, investors in government bonds, holders of mortgages, owners of life insurance, savings depositors—are repaid in coin of less purchasing power than they lent. Small savers in particular do not realize the risks they run in acquiring fixed-money-value assets and need to be protected from these risks. Investors with more wealth and better information are able to hedge against inflation by investing in common stocks or other claims to real property. It is a major defect of our financial structure that inflation hedges are not available for the majority of the population; American inventiveness and ingenuity have been sadly lacking in this area. The government could issue bonds with purchasing-power guarantees, and life insurance companies could offer "variable" annuities to protect beneficiaries against inflation. Some of the energy spent in denouncing inflation—and the more difficult it seems to be to control, the more loudly it is denounced—could better be spent in designing institutions that mitigate its inequities. It would not be hard to make inflation innocuous even to investors of limited means and knowledge.

The main inflationary consequences of government expenditure can and should be avoided by resolute taxation. But even if the budget is balanced, inflation may result from an excess of private demands over the resources available to satisfy them or from private pressures for increasing money incomes at rates excessive in relation to the growth of productivity.

The Federal Reserve System can fight inflation with "tight money"; and beginning in 1956, we have been sacrificing some production, and some growth in our productive capacity, to the anti-inflationary objectives of the Administration and the Federal Reserve. The evidences of the sacrifice are numerous: increasing unemployment, reduction in weekly hours of work and in overtime, withdrawal of women and young people from the labor force, retardation of the rate of growth of total output, decline of industrial production, excess capacity in steel and other industries. The Federal Reserve has deliberately kept credit tight enough to produce some slack in the economy, in the hope that the rate of price increase (running at 3 or 4 per cent per year) will be moderated. So far this hope has not been justified, and indeed it is not clear that the main sources of the inflation are vulnerable to any weapons at the disposal of the Federal Reserve. No one but Mr. Martin knows how much slack the Federal Reserve is willing to force upon the economy in the effort to stop inflation. Even after the Federal Reserve gave, in November 1957, belated recognition to the recession all other observers detected months before, its actions were mainly passive and symbolic. By the end of January, the "Fed" had yet to give the banks a significant transfusion of new reserves to enable them to increase their lending.

It is true that tight money weeds out many highly dispensable uses of resources; to a certain extent the more urgent needs are the ones that can pay the higher interest rates and qualify for credit accommodation. But the victims of tight money are also public investment programs—in education, public health, urban redevelopment—that the nation can ill afford to postpone. Some mechanism for moderating these effects of tight money is urgently needed.

The American people have entrusted military judgments to the military man they have installed in the White House. When all else fails, the defense budget is defended against critical attacks from both directions by appeal to his authority. President Eisenhower would not take chances with the nation's security. President Eisenhower would not say we needed so large a budget unless we really do. Whatever one may think of the President's ability to assess our military and diplomatic position, these appeals to his authority omit the other half of the considerations relevant to his budgetary decisions. If it is a question of cutting the defense budget, the risks to our security and to the position of the free world must be balanced against the gains to our economy and to our civilian standard of life. If it is a question of increasing the defense budget, the improvements in our military and diplomatic position must be weighed against the losses to our private economy and our consumption standards. Even if President Eisenhower is a reliable expert on the military side of this balance, no one has suggested that he is an authority on the economic side. Concerning the seriousness of changes in the budget for the short-run and long-run vigor of the economy and well-being of the population, he has relied on Secretary Humphrey. The result is that he has greatly overestimated the weight of the considerations that oppose defense spending and other governmental programs.

The President's budget for 1958–59 shows the continuing force of this tragic overestimate. Though billed in headlines as the largest peacetime budget ever, it actually represents a reduction in the physical volume of goods and services to be purchased by the government. This is true both of the budget as a whole and of its defense component. The illusion of increase is due to rises in the costs of the goods and services the government buys. The budget means a smaller flow of product to the federal government in absolute terms, and it means an even greater reduction in the government's relative share of our growing national capacity to produce. Public concern has prodded a reluctant President to propose modest increases in spending for missiles and other new weapons, foreign aid, federal scholarships, and scientific research. But in his view these increases must be met by curtailments of other federal programs, mostly other defense programs. If he must request federal money for scholarships and science, then he evidently feels he cannot ask again for funds for school construction. The President does not consider the possibility that many private uses of resources might be much more logical candidates for sacrifice than governmental programs, defense or non-defense. Indeed his budget leaves the way clear for *all* of the growing capacity of the economy to be channeled into still further elevation of our standards of luxury.

The American people, it is often said, don't want to pay the enormous costs of national security. They are not willing, it is said, to pay the taxes necessary to keep the Western world ahead in basic science, in weapons research and development, in armaments in being. They are tired, it is alleged, of the drain on their resources involved in our peaceful competition with Communism for the economic development of the new nations of Africa and Asia.

What the American people decide they want depends on how well their leaders inform them about the dangers the country and the world face. They have gladly acquiesced in the mood of complacency and indulgence fostered by the Eisenhower Administration. But their entire history leaves no doubt that they would also rise to a challenge frankly presented by a leadership genuinely alert to the dangers confronting the free world. The Russian satellites may shake the American people from their complacency and cause them to demand the kind of leadership that elected democratic leaders are supposed to provide without prompting from their followers. Sputnik will be well worth the blow it has dealt our national pride if it frees national policy from the shackles of fiscal orthodoxy. The Treasury and Defense Departments are under new leaders, like their predecessors men who have demonstrated their capabilities for practical leadership in private affairs. If they carry to their new jobs the pragmatic approach that led to their private success, our policy may yet be determined by the needs of the age rather than by ancient ideology.

Chapter 7

On the Economic Burden of Defense

The oceans no longer guarantee the North American continent immunity from military attack, and nothing seems likely to take their place. Absolute security is a thing of the past; and the imperfect and uncertain defenses now available to us are, unlike the natural barriers that once protected us, very, very expensive. I propose here to discuss some of the economic implications of this revolution. I shall consider first the effects on the domestic economy, and second the profound change in the international economic position of the United States.

The security of the nation costs roughly one tenth of our Gross National Product every year. I count this as a burden, but I know that some critics of American capitalism argue that it is not. There are two versions of the argument that defense production is really free—one that the resources devoted to defense would simply be unemployed otherwise, the other that they would be wasted in frivolities and luxuries our society could well do without. I shall take up these two versions in turn.

According to the first view, it is only the stimulus of defense demand that has kept the U.S. economy from relapsing into the mass unemployment and stagnation of the 'thirties. In the absence of this stimulus, not only would the labor now employed to make and man armaments, be unemployed, but many other workers, through indirect effects, would be out of their jobs also. The industrial capacity now committed to armament either would lie idle or would never have come into being.

Originally published in *Reports and Speeches of the Eighth Yale Conference on the Teaching of the Social Studies* (Yale University Graduate School, April 1963).

History has not performed this experiment for us. But the evidence is against so pessimistic an assessment of the vitality of our economic and political system. Although defense expenditures have been high by historical standards ever since the Second World War, we have taken in stride two cutbacks in military spending—one spectacular reduction immediately after the war, amounting to $65 billion, over one quarter of GNP, and a second, amounting to $10 billion, nearly 3 per cent of GNP, in the first Eisenhower Administration following the Korean settlement. During the first postwar decade our primary economic problem was much more typically excess demand and inflation than inadequate demand and unemployment. If the defense program was really a mammoth WPA, we were surely overdoing it.

The American people have taxed themselves heavily to pay for defense, suppressing private consumption in order to make room in the economy for defense production. In 1929 consumption took 75 per cent of GNP; now it takes 65 per cent. The number of federal personal income taxpayers has increased twentyfold, and the rates they pay, which ranged from ⅜ of 1 per cent to 24 per cent in 1929, now start at 20 per cent and rise to 91 per cent. Without the defense burden our taxes would be much lower, our private consumption spending higher, and our civilian public expenditures higher too.

The germ of truth in the view I am discussing lies in the politics and ideology, rather than the economics, of government budgets. The sheer size of defense expenditures even when they are matched dollar for dollar by taxes, is an expansionary economic influence. The reason is that taxes are paid at the expense of saving as well as spending. To put the point another way, if government expenditures were lowered by, say, $25 billion (about half the present defense budget) it would be necessary to cut tax receipts by more than $25 billion—perhaps $30 billion—in order to induce taxpayers to replace the $25 billion of government spending with $25 billion of their own spending. This means that if government expenditures were substantially lower, we would probably need *more* frequent and *larger* budget deficits to maintain prosperity and high employment.

There is nothing frightening about this conclusion except that it is so poorly understood in this country. If we must assume that the balanced-budget fetish would have ruled fiscal policy regardless of the consequences for the economy, then economists do have cause to be thankful for high defense expenditures. These outlays have made the fetish less damaging than it would have been with small government budgets. Indeed, through much of the postwar period the urge to balance the federal budget has helped to contain inflationary pressures. The renewed popularity of the balanced-budget principle since the war is probably in some degree an adaptation to this situation.

From an economic standpoint, it is perfectly feasible, through proper fiscal and monetary policy, to sustain prosperity and high employment with much smaller government expenditures. I am optimistic enough about American democracy to believe that the political and ideological obstacles to the use of such policies would melt away if circumstances were obviously and persistently different from those of 1947–57—less danger of inflation, more threat of unemployment and excess capacity. After all, the experience of the 'thirties led the American people to resolve solemnly, in the Employment Act of 1946, that their government would never again sit idly by and permit large-scale unemployment and depression.

I have been discussing the view that defense has not been an economic burden, because the manpower and the other productive resources devoted to it—and perhaps many more—would have been unemployed otherwise. There is a second line of reasoning that might lead to a similar conclusion, namely that if these resources were not actually idle, at any rate they would be wasted. They would be producing socially useless goods and services. Affluent America, in this view, is already saturated with consumption goods. The nation can keep its vastly efficient, increasingly automated, productive machine occupied only by continuously creating artificial wants—wants for things that the same process soon renders obsolete. Keeping up with the Russians in missiles is just a substitute for keeping up with the Joneses in advertised gadgets.

Without doubt trivia and status symbols are a large component of U.S. private consumption. But economic progress has always been a race between productivity, on the one hand, and rising standards and aspirations, on the other. There is no reason to believe we have won that race today, any more than we had won it in the New Era of the 'twenties. As social scientists, we are inclined to believe we can never really win it.

Certainly a look at the incomes and consumption patterns of a large part of the American population today should disabuse any observer of the illusion that consumption levels cannot be usefully increased. Americans do not exhibit by their behavior any signs of saturation. Married women, teenagers, retired people seek jobs when they can. Breadwinners cherish the opportunity to work overtime and even to engage in "moonlighting." Americans spend, as they consistently have done, about 93 per cent of their earnings after taxes. They seek to improve their houses, to see the country and the world, to camp and to boat, to buy paperbacks and high-fidelity records, to improve their health and medical care, to fix and straighten their children's teeth, and to send the children in droves to colleges. To the extent that defense has been purchased at the expense of private consumption, it has not been free but has been a real burden on the nation.

It is easy to see why civilian government has suffered from the defense program. Defense is a government activity, and the economies it entails fall naturally on other government activities. Since defense makes government budgets frighteningly large and taxes unpleasantly high, political instincts and pressures work to restrain the growth of other government activities and of revenues to finance them. The nation can well afford expansion of these activities, many of which deserve higher priority than the private activities with which they compete for resources. But we are accustomed to looking narrowly at what government can afford, instead of broadly at what the nation can afford. Thus President Kennedy has found it necessary to give the economy its much-needed boost by cutting taxes to encourage private spending rather than by increasing non-defense spending. No other course is politically feasible, and the President must couple his plea for tax reduction with a pledge to keep civilian government expenditures in check. I think it is fair to conclude that in the absence of the defense program there would be more funds, at all levels of government, for schools, colleges, hospitals, roads, parks, urban rehabilitation, urban transport, and social welfare.

There is another sense in which the defense effort may have been an economic cost to the American people, but it is difficult to assess. Has the concentration of research and development efforts on defense slowed down the rate of technical progress in civilian production? Research and development have become bywords in American industry since the war, and we have increased dramatically our expenditures for these purposes, until they now amount to about 3 per cent of GNP. But most of this is oriented to defense. Half of it is federally financed, and a large share of the privately financed effort occurs in defense and space industries. Most of the scientific and technological talent of the country is devoting itself to building better weapons rather than better mousetraps. Although there is undoubtedly some spillover —new techniques and products designed for defense purposes turn out to have civilian uses too—it is not easy to find examples. Clearly the same mobilization of talent and resources to improve civilian productivity would have set us much farther ahead.

On the other hand it is equally clear that this is not a real alternative—we just do not set up Manhattan Projects to solve problems like suburban commutation and urban congestion. If the defense effort has monopolized physicists and engineers, it has also induced a faster increase in their supply. Sputnik appears to have set off a slow revolution in the quality of American education, which eventually may turn out to contribute greatly to our national well-being as well as to our national strength.

The postwar rate of growth in productivity in the economy as a whole has been within the range of normal historical experience. I find it difficult to assign the defense effort either a plus or a minus on this score.

I have discussed some of the major domestic economic consequences of the passing of the age of free security. I turn now to some of the consequences for the external economic position of the United States. There the revolution in military technology has had dramatic effects, particularly on our economic relations with Western Europe.

Before the Second World War Europe was militarily and politically vulnerable. The United States was not. The United States was the safe haven for property, and our vaults filled with the world's gold as money was invested here for safekeeping. This consideration overrode normal economic calculations of profitability. Now Western Europe is as safe as America; the differential risk that led to concentration of capital in dollar assets has vanished. Europe has reclaimed its natural economic share of the investments of its own citizens, and of Americans and others as well. As a result, much of the gold that fled to this country in the 'thirties and 'forties has departed.

The process has been painful to us in many ways. We became accustomed to thinking of the dollar as unique among national currencies, and of all other currencies as funny money. Now we find that other currencies—Deutschemarks or francs or guilders or Swiss francs—can be strong too, and since currency strength is purely relative, their strength makes the dollar look weak. More important, the reversal of capital movements in favor of Europe has hampered our domestic economic policy. Accustomed to pursuing fiscal and monetary policies for domestic objectives alone, we now find that we must worry about the effects of our policies on our balance of payments and our gold reserves. This has long been an everyday preoccupation of our European friends, but it is new to us and somewhat mysterious. We are not, in fact, as free as we were before to adopt expansionary measures to stimulate the domestic economy. And we overreact in fear of the unknown—warnings about "gold losses," "loss of confidence in the dollar," and the balance-of-payments deficit are potent new weapons in the hands of financial conservatives who always oppose expansionary policies anyway.

The same revolution in military technology has reversed the world roles of the United States and Europe. Formerly, we were sheltered by the British navy, and in a sense by the French army. Today our nuclear deterrent and our armed presence shelter Western Europe. We cannot guarantee their security any more than our own, but the security we do provide comes at little cost to Europe itself. At the same time, the U.S. has of necessity assumed many of the former responsibilities of Europe toward the rest of the world, all the more difficult and expensive because of the Cold War, the breakup of colonialism, and the aspirations of the new nations for rapid economic development.

These reversals of role have signaled a decline in Europe's power and political influence in the world, but they have been accompanied by the most remarkable economic progress within Europe since before 1913. Relatively unburdened by defense and released from overseas commitments (France must be excepted on both counts), most European economies have grown much faster than our own since 1950. European exporters have strengthened their competitive positions in world markets. The move toward continental European unity, of which the Common Market is the principal achievement, may be seen as a compensation for the decline in European political power in the world. We have supported it for political reasons, but it is making life more difficult for our exporters, especially our farmers, and it is another factor encouraging the flow of investment capital to Europe. Meanwhile our defense and foreign aid activities have poured billions of dollars overseas. Many of these dollars have come into the possession of European central bankers who can and sometimes do exchange them at the U.S. Treasury for gold. Here is another way in which the new military situation has weakened the international monetary position of the United States.

This is not a calamity, and I do not mean to exaggerate its importance. Monetary arrangements are means, not ends; and the external position of the dollar or any currency is not of such overriding importance as bankers and central bankers are disposed and obliged to believe. We are certainly wealthy and productive enough to afford troops in Germany, bases in Italy, and aid to India—even if they do require us to buy, directly or indirectly, European currencies with dollars. We still sell more goods abroad than we buy. Our balance-of-payments deficit, troublesome as it is, amounts to less than ½ of 1 per cent of our Gross National Product and essentially reflects the exchange of gold and short-term debt for less liquid but more remunerative and productive assets abroad. The chronic glut of dollars is likely to be no more permanent than the dollar shortage that preceded it.

Meanwhile, however, we face the difficult task of adapting to a new and more symmetrical world monetary situation. The dollar has been serving as an international currency, and the United States has been the world's banker. These functions will be shared more and more with Europe, and more and more internationalized. In this, as in other respects, the military revolution has brought the United States down to earth, subject to the same burdens, frustrations, and problems as the ordinary run of mortal nations.

Chapter 8

Growth Through Taxation

The overriding issue of political economy in the 1960s is how to allocate the national output. How much to private consumption? How much for private investment in plant and equipment? For government investment and public services? For national defense? For foreign aid and overseas investment? Though our productive capacity is great and is growing, the demands upon it seem to be growing even faster.

The allocation of resources among competing uses is *the* central and classical theoretical problem of economics. Likewise it is the inescapable central practical problem of a Soviet-type planned economy, or of any economy under the forced draft of total war. Only recently has allocation of the output of the peacetime American economy begun to emerge from economics texts into the political arena, as a challenge and opportunity for democratic decision and governmental action. Public economic policy and debate have long been dominated by other concerns: unemployment, inflation, inequality. The composition of national output has been an unintended by-product rather than a conscious objective of economic policy.

The importance of accelerating economic growth brings the question of allocation to the fore. Can we as a nation, by political decision and governmental action, increase our rate of growth? Or must the rate of growth be regarded fatalistically, the result of uncoordinated decisions and habits of millions of consumers, businessmen, and governments, uncontrollable in our kind of society except by exhortation and prayer? The Communists are

Originally published in *The New Republic* (July 25, 1960), pp. 15–18.

telling the world that they alone know how to mobilize economic resources for rapid growth. The appeal of free institutions in the underdeveloped world, and perhaps even their survival in the West, may depend on whether the Communists are right. We cannot, we need not, leave the outcome to chance.

How can an increase in the rate of growth of national output be achieved? The answer is straightforward and painful. We must devote more of our current capacity to uses that increase our future capacity, and correspondingly less to other uses. The uses of current capacity that build up future productive capacity are of three major types: (1) *Investment:* replacement and expansion of the country's stock of productive capital—factories, machines, roads, trucks, school buildings, hospitals, power dams, pipelines. (2) *Research,* both in basic science and in industrial application, by government, private industry, and nonprofit institutions, leading sooner or later to more efficient processes and new products. (3) *Education* of all kinds augmenting the skill of the future labor force. The competing uses of current capacity are: (1) *Unemployment:* failure to employ current capacity to the full, thus losing potential production. (2) *Consumption,* where most of our resources are engaged, providing us with the goods, services, and leisure that constitute the most luxurious standard of living the world has known.

Since 1953 the economy has been operating at an average unemployment level of 4.9 per cent of the labor force, and the Eisenhower Administration seems to regard 5 per cent as a highly satisfactory boom-time performance. A society geared to the objective of growth should keep the average unemployment rate down to 3 per cent. Reduction of unemployment to this level could increase Gross National Product from the current labor force and capital stock by about $20 billion. But this increase in output will contribute to economic growth only if it is used in substantial part for investment, research, and education; it will make no contribution if it is all consumed. Republican economic policies are highly vulnerable. But critics should eschew the superficial political appeal of the unfounded line that more vigorous pursuit of full employment, with a battery of New Deal antidepression remedies, will by itself assure rapid growth.

To stimulate growth we must somehow engineer two shifts in the composition of actual and potential national output. One is from private consumption to the public sector, federal, state, and local. Domestic economic growth is, of course, not the only reason for such a shift. Increased defense, increased foreign aid, increased public consumption are possibly equally urgent reasons. The second shift of resources that must be engineered is from private consumption to private investment. About three-quarters of Gross National Product is produced with the help of business plant and equipment. Faster growth of output requires a more rapidly expanding and more up-to-date stock of plant and equipment. Every $1.00 increase of GNP requires in the neighborhood of $1.50 new plant and equipment investment. Thus to raise the rate of growth 2 percentage points, say from 3 per cent to 5 per cent per annum, the share of plant and equipment investment in current GNP must rise by 3 percentage points, e.g. from 10 to 13 per cent.

Tables 8.1 and 8.2 provide a concrete illustration of the kind of change we need in the relative composition of output if we are serious about increasing our rate of growth. Table 8.1 shows the actual composition of GNP in 1953 and 1959 and a suggested target for 1965. Table 8.2 shows the composition of GNP in the three years with correction for price changes, i.e. in "constant 1959 dollars." Table 8.4 is based on Tables 8.1 and 8.2 but brings out the essential point more clearly. It shows how the actual increase in GNP between 1953 and 1959 was allocated among major uses and, in contrast, how we should allocate the growth in output over the next six years if we really want output to grow.

Between 1953 and 1959 potential GNP rose from $365 billion to an estimated $500 billion. The composition of GNP in these years is shown in Table 8.1. The way in which the $135 billion increase was used is shown in the first column of Table 8.4. Some of the potential increase went to waste in unemployment. Of the realized increase, 69 per cent went into consumption, 13 per cent into government activity, and 18 per cent into investment. Unfortunately these calculations *understate* the effective growth of consumption relative to government and investment. The reason is that the prices of goods and services needed for government

Table 8.1. Composition of Gross National Product in Current Dollars

	1953	1959	1965 target
		(billions of dollars)	
Potential Gross National Product (3% unemployment)	365	500 (104%)	688*
Actual Gross National Product	365 (100%)	479 (100%)	688 (100%)
Private consumption	233 (64%)	311 (65%)	390 (58%)
Government purchases of goods and services	83 (23%)	98 (20%)	173 (25%)
a. Privately produced	51 (14%)	53 (11%)	88 (13%)
b. Services of government employees	32 (9%)	45 (9%)	85 (12%)
Gross private investment	50 (14%)	70 (15%)	125 (18%)
a. Plant and equipment	36 (10%)	44 (9%)	88 (13%)
b. Increase in inventories	—	4 (1%)	8 (1%)
c. Residential construction	14 (4%)	22 (5%)	27 (4%)
Net private foreign investment	-1 —	-1 —	0 (0%)

Source for actual data 1953 and 1959: *Economic Report of the President, 1960.*

*The Council of Economic Advisers now (July 1965) estimates potential GNP for 1965 in current dollars, for 4 per cent unemployment, at $684 billion. However, prices have risen more than I assumed in the tables; consumption prices have risen about 8 per cent since 1959 instead of remaining stationary.

Table 8.2. Composition of Gross National Product in Constant 1959 Dollars

	1953	1959	1965 target
		(billions of dollars)	
Potential Gross National Product (3% unemployment)	417	500 (104%)	650*
Actual Gross National Product	417 (100%)	479 (100%)	650 (100%)
Private consumption	254 (61%)	311 (65%)	390 (60%)
Government purchases of goods and services	102 (24%)	98 (20%)	145 (22%)
a. Privately produced	59 (14%)	53 (11%)	80 (12%)
b. Services of government employees	43 (10%)	45 (9%)	65 (10%)
Gross private investment	60 (15%)	70 (15%)	115 (18%)
a. Plant and equipment	44 (11%)	44 (9%)	80 (12%)
b. Increase in inventories	1 —	4 (1%)	8 (1%)
c. Residential construction	15 (4%)	22 (5%)	27 (4%)
Net private foreign investment	1 —	-1 —	0 (0%)

Source for actual data 1953 and 1959: *Economic Report of the President, 1960.*

*(July 1965): The Council of Economic Advisers estimate of potential GNP for 1965 at 4 per cent unemployment is $630 billion in 1959 dollars. For 3 per cent unemployment it would be perhaps $640 billion. The difference from my $650 billion target reflects the low investment of the intervening years. But the difference is small and suggests that I underestimated the growth of the economy in the absence of the measures I advocated and, by the same token, probably overestimated their ability to add to the growth rate.

activity and private investment rose relative to the prices of consumption goods and services. The extent of price increases for the various components of GNP is shown in Table 8.3. For example, the services of government employees (teachers, policemen, clerks, etc.) rose in price 34 per cent while consumer prices rose 9 per cent. Although we managed to increase government expenditure for such services by $13 billion, $11 billion of the increase was simply the higher cost of the volume of services we were already getting in 1953 and only $2 billion represented a real expansion of such services. When account is taken of this and other unfavorable relative price changes, some 92 per cent of the growth in output "in constant dollars" went to consumption; government activity actually diminished; private investment got 16 per cent of the increase in GNP, and none of this increase was for plant and equipment. (See column 3 of Table 8.4.)

Unfortunately we will probably have to continue to do some running just to stay in the same place. The target suggested for 1965 in Tables 8.1 and 8.2 assumes that prices of goods and services for investment will rise, relative to consumer prices, in the proportions shown in Table 8.3. If consumption prices are kept stable from 1959 to 1965, potential 1965 GNP is estimated at $688 billion. Table 8.1 suggests that we resolve to increase to

Table 8.3. Price Increases of GNP Components

	Actual: 1959 prices relative to 1953	Assumed: 1965 prices relative to 1959
Private consumption	1.09	1.00
Government purchases of goods and services		
a. Privately produced	1.15	1.10
b. Services of government employees	1.34	1.30
Gross private investment		
a. Plant and equipment	1.22	1.10
b. Residential construction	1.07	1.05

Table 8.4. Disposition of Increases in GNP

	Current Dollars		Constant 1959 Dollars	
	1953 to 1959	1959 to 1965	1953 to 1959	1959 to 1965
	(billions of dollars)			
Potential Gross National Product	135 (118%)	188 (90%)	83 (133%)	150 (88%)
Actual Gross National Product	114 (100%)	209 (100%)	62 (100%)	171 (100%)
Private consumption	78 (69%)	79 (38%)	57 (92%)	79 (46%)
Government purchases of goods and services	15 (13%)	75 (36%)	−4 (−6%)	47 (27%)
a. Privately produced	2 (2%)	35 (17%)	−6 (−10%)	27 (16%)
b. Services of government employees	13 (11%)	40 (19%)	2 (3%)	20 (11%)
Gross private investment	20 (18%)	55 (26%)	10 (16%)	45 (26%)
a. Plant and equipment	8 (7%)	44 (21%)	0 (0%)	36 (21%)
b. Increase in inventories	4 (5%)	4 (2%)	3 (5%)	4 (2%)
c. Residential construction	8 (7%)	7 (3%)	7 (11%)	5 (3%)
Net private foreign investment	—	—	−1 (−2%)	1 —

25 per cent the government share of that output, and to 18 per cent the investment share. The assumed price increases in those sectors would nullify part of those increases, leaving us a GNP of $650 billion in constant 1959 dollars, with the composition shown in Table 8.2. In order to keep from consuming more than 46 per cent of the projected increase in real output we must restrain consumption to 38 per cent of the growth of dollar output. (See Table 8.4.)

Policy to accelerate growth must be double-edged. On the one hand, it must stimulate the desired government and private expenditures. On the other, it must discourage consumption. Here are some major constituents of a program for growth:

1. Increased expenditure by federal, state, and local governments for education, basic and applied research, urban redevelopment, resource conservation and development, transportation, and other public facilities.

2. Stimulus to private investment expenditures by:
   a. Federal Reserve and Treasury policy to create and maintain "easy money" conditions, with credit readily available and interest rates low, especially in long-term capital markets.
   b. Improvement of averaging and loss-offset provisions in taxation of corporate income, in order to increase the degree to which the tax collector shares the risk of investment as well as the reward.
   c. The privilege of deducting from corporate net income for tax purposes a certain percentage of a corporation's outlays for plant and equipment to the extent that these outlays exceed a specified minimum. The specified minimum would be the sum of depreciation and (on the assumption that the tax rate is 52 per cent) 48 per cent of net income before tax. To qualify for the tax concession, a corporation would have to be investing more than its normal gross profits after tax. The concession, and the minimum requirement for eligibility for it, are designed to encourage greater corporate saving, the full investment of internal funds, and, most important, the

undertaking of investment financed by outside saving obtained from the capital market. An analogous proposal to encourage noncorporate saving and investment is suggested below.

If these measures were adopted, a reduction in the basic corporate income tax rate, advocated by many as essential to growth, would be neither necessary nor equitable. Indeed the strength of these measures might be greater if the rate were increased.

3. Restriction of consumption, by:
   a. Increase in personal income tax at all levels, accompanied by permission to deduct a certain amount of saving from income subject to tax. Like present deductions for charity or medical care, the saving deduction would be claimed at the taxpayer's option, with the burden of proof on him. A schedule of "normal" saving for taxpayers of various incomes and family circumstances would be established, and only saving in excess of a taxpayer's "normal" would be eligible for deduction. A scheme of this kind seems to be the most feasible equitable way to use the tax instrument to favor saving at the expense of consumption.[2]
   b. Improvements in the Social Security system—e.g. raising retirement benefits and relating their amount, above a common minimum, to cumulated covered earnings— should be introduced on a quasi-contributory basis. Since the payroll tax contributions then precede the benefits, the funds accumulate and can be an important channel of national saving.
   c. Increases in state and local taxes—property or sales or income as the case may be—to keep pace with the share of these governments in the necessary expansion of the public sector.
   d. Limitation, to a reasonable proportion of sales, of the privilege of deducting advertising and promotional ex-

2. For a further discussion of this proposal, see James Tobin, "Taxes, Saving, and Inflation," *American Economic Review, 39* (December 1949), 1223–32.

penses from corporate income subject to tax. No observer of the American scene doubts that advertising is excessive. From the economic point of view, it absorbs too large a share of the nation's resources itself, and at the same time it generates synthetic pressures for ever-higher consumption.

Increased taxation is the price of growth. We must tax ourselves not only to finance the necessary increase in public expenditures but also to finance, indirectly, the expansion of private investment. A federal budget surplus is a method by which we as a nation can expand the volume of saving available for private investment beyond the current saving of individuals and corporations. The surplus must, to be sure, be coupled with measures to stimulate investment, so that the national resolution to save actually leads to capital formation and is not wasted in unemployment and unrequited loss of consumption. It is only superficially paradoxical to combine anti-inflationary fiscal policy with an expansionary monetary policy. The policies outlined above must be combined in the right proportions, so that aggregate demand is high enough to maintain a 3 per cent unemployment rate but not higher. There are several mixtures that can do that job; of them we must choose the one that gives the desired composition of aggregate demand. If the overwhelming problem of democratic capitalism in the '30s and even the '50s was to bring the business cycle under social control, the challenge of the '60s is to bring under public decision the broad allocation of national output. Fortunately the means are at hand. They are techniques well within the peacetime scope of government. We can do the job without the direct controls of wartime—priorities, rationing, price and wage controls.

The means are at hand; to use them we will need to muster more wisdom, maturity, leadership, and sense of national purpose than we displayed in the '50s. A program like the suggested 1965 target, which allows an increase of per capita consumption at about 1 per cent a year, is scarcely a program of austerity. Indeed it would not feel austere even if the growth of gross output per head were held to $1\frac{1}{2}$ per cent per annum. We are used to institutions that let us realize in increased consumption about two thirds of increases in output. But let people earn the incomes associated with a 2½ per cent rise in output per capita, and the measures necessary to keep their consumption from rising faster than 1 per cent may seem burdensome sacrifices. Our Communist competitors have an advantage. Since they do not pay out such increases in output as personal incomes in the first place, they do not have the problem of recapturing them in taxes or saving. That problem we cannot escape in a free society. Unless we master it, we shall not fare well in the competition for economic growth and national survival.

Chapter 9

Economic Growth as an Objective of Government Policy

In recent years economic growth has come to occupy an exalted position in the hierarchy of goals of government policy, both in the United States and abroad, both in advanced and in less developed countries, both in centrally controlled and decentralized economies. National governments proclaim target growth rates for such diverse economies as the Soviet Union, Yugoslavia, India, Sweden, France, Japan—and even for the United Kingdom and the United States, where the targets indicate dissatisfaction with past performance. Growth is an international goal, too. The Organization for Economic Cooperation and Development aims at a 50 per cent increase in the collective gross output of the Atlantic Community over the current decade.

Growth has become a good word. And the better a word becomes, the more it is invoked to bless a variety of causes and the more it loses specific meaning. At least in professional economic discussion, we need to give a definite and distinctive meaning to growth as a policy objective. Let it be neither a new synonym for good things in general nor a fashionable way to describe other economic objectives. Let growth be something it is possible to oppose as well as to favor, depending on judgments of social priorities and opportunities.

In essence the question of growth is nothing new, but a new disguise for an age-old issue, one which has always intrigued and preoccupied economists: the present versus the future.

Originally published in *American Economic Review, Papers and Proceedings, 54* (May 1964), 1–20.

How should society divide its resources between current needs and pleasures and those of next year, next decade, next generation?

The choice can be formalized in a way that makes clear what is essentially at stake. A consumption path or program for an economy describes its rate of consumption at every time point beginning now and extending indefinitely into the future. Not all imaginable consumption paths are feasible. At any moment future possibilities are limited by our inherited stocks of productive resources and technological knowledge and by our prospects for autonomous future increase in these stocks. Of feasible paths, some dominate others, i.e. path A dominates B if consumption along path A exceeds consumption along path B at every point of time. I hope I will incur no one's wrath by asserting that in almost everyone's value scheme more is better than less (or certainly not worse), at least if we are careful to specify more or less of what. If this assertion is accepted, the interesting choices are between undominated or efficient feasible paths, i.e. between a pair A and C where A promises more consumption at some points in time but less at others. See Figure 9.1. In particular, I take growthmanship to be advocacy of paths that promise more consumption later in return for less earlier.

But growthmanship means more than that. Growthmen are usually willing to throw the weight of the government on to the scales in order to tip the balance in favor of the future. Here they fly in the face of a doctrinal tradition of considerable strength both in economics and in popular ideology. Does not the market so coordinate the free, decentralized decisions of individuals between present and future so as to reach an optimal social choice? Is not any government intervention in favor of growth, therefore, bound to tilt the scales toward the future to a degree that society does not "really" want?

The basic question raised by advocates of faster growth may be further formalized to emphasize this issue. Assuming that the economy is now on a feasible and undominated consumption path, the desirability of deviating from it can be expressed in the language of interest rates and present values. Any feasible and efficient path, including the prevailing path, implies two sets of interest rates. One, which we may call the time preference set, expresses the society's marginal rates of substitution as consumers between consumption at one date and consumption at another date. This set answers questions like the following: Given society's consumption prospect, how much increase in consumption five years or fifty years or t years from now is

Figure 9.1. *Alternative Consumption Paths*

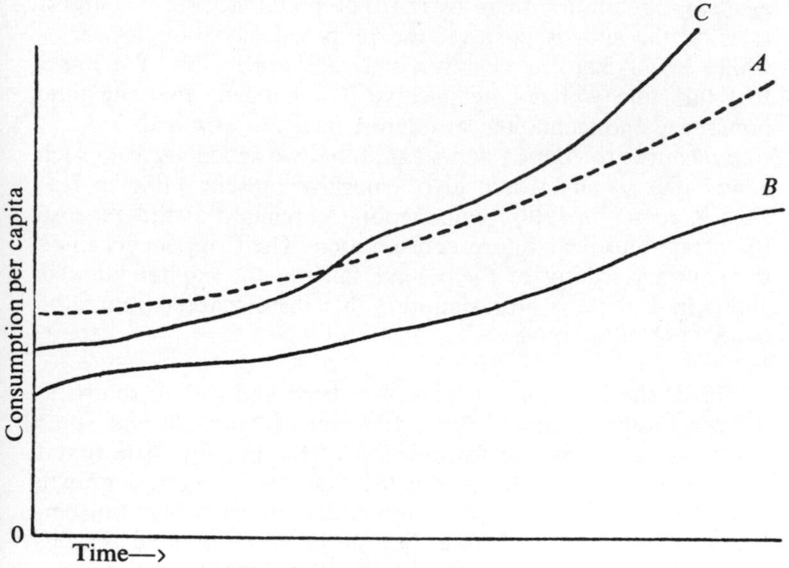

A dominates B but not C.

worth the loss of a dollar's worth of consumption today? The rates implied by the answers need not all be the same. The other set, which we may call the technological set, expresses the opportunities that present and prospective technology offers the society for marginal substitutions of consumption at one date for consumption at another. This set answers questions like the following: Given the consumption path, by how much could consumption be increased five years or fifty years or t years from now by the resources released from a dollar's worth of consumption today? Again, the rates can vary with time. A sacrifice in current consumption may yield, say, 10 per cent per year if its fruits are taken five years from now, but 20 per cent—or 2 per cent—if they are taken fifty years from now.

A small proposed feasible deviation from the existing path can in principle be tested as follows: Calculate the present values of the proposed deviations in consumption, negative and positive, discounting them by the time preference set of interest rates. If the sum is positive, the proposed deviation is worthwhile. If it is zero or negative, it is not worthwhile. We know that this sum will not be positive if it happens that the time preference and technological interest rates are identical.

Evidently growthmen believe that the two sets diverge in such a way that society would give a positive present value to feasible increases in future consumption purchased at the expense of current and near-future consumption. Their opponents think the contrary. Many of them have faith in the capital markets and believe there is a presumption that these markets make the two sets of rates equal.

This is the heart of the issue, I believe, and I shall return to it later in this chapter. First, however, I must discuss some questions raised by the formulation of the growth issue that I have just tried to sketch. What is the relationship between growth and other objectives of economic policy, in particular full employment of resources? Are there some noneconomic reasons for accelerating growth—reasons that this formulation excludes or evades? Exactly what is the "consumption" whose path is to be chosen? Finally, can government successfully influence the growth path?

Growth Versus Full Employment

To accelerate growth is not the same thing as to increase the utilization of existing resources, manpower, and capital capacity. In the formulation sketched above, a consumption path with underutilization is dominated or inefficient. By putting the idle resources to work, consumption can be increased both now and in future. The same is true of other measures to improve the efficiency of allocation of resources. We can all agree, I presume, on the desirability of growth measures free of any cost. If that is the meaning of growth policy, there is no issue.

For short periods of time, stepping up the utilization of capacity can increase the recorded rate of growth of output and consumption. But over the decades fluctuations in the utilization of capacity will have a minor influence compared to the growth of capacity itself. To express the same point somewhat differently, the subject of economic growth refers mainly to supply, or capacity to produce, rather than to demand. In the short run, accelerating the growth of demand for goods and services can, by increasing the rate of utilization of capacity, speed the growth of output. But in the long run, output and real demand cannot grow faster than capacity. If monetary demand is made to set a faster pace, it will be frustrated by a rate of inflation that cuts real demand down to size.

Public policy affecting aggregate demand should be aimed at maintaining a desired rate of utilization of capacity. Economists and other citizens will differ on how high this rate should be, because they differ in the weights they attach to additional employment and output, on the one hand, and to the risks of faster price inflation, on the other. But however this balance is struck, monetary and fiscal policies can in principle hit the target utilization rate just as well whether the economy's capacity is growing at 5 per cent or 3 per cent or zero per cent.

Full employment is, therefore, not a reason for faster economic growth; each is an objective in its own right. In an economy suffering from low rates of utilization of manpower and capital resources, accelerating the growth of aggregate demand may well be the need of the hour. But this ought not be considered growth policy in the more fundamental sense. Tax reduction today has sufficient justification as a means of expanding demand and raising the rate of utilization. It is probably an unfortunate confusion to bill it as a growth measure, too.

I do not mean, of course, that the rate of growth of the economy's capacity is in practice wholly independent of its rate of utilization. In principle they may be independent. Demand can be expanded in ways that do not accelerate, indeed may even retard, the growth in capacity itself. But as a rule some of the output resulting from an increase in utilization will be used in ways that expand future capacity. Thus the Great Depression deprived the nation and the world of investment as well as consumption; we, as well as our fathers, bear the cost. The proposed tax reduction, even though its major impact is to stimulate consumption, will nonetheless increase the share of national capacity devoted to capital accumulation. It is in this sense that it can be called a growth measure. But there may be ways to expand demand and utilization to the same degree while at the same time providing both more stimulus for and more economic room for capacity-building uses of resources now idle.

Noneconomic Reasons for Growth

Economic growth may be a national objective for noneconomic reasons, for national prestige or national strength or national purpose.

No doubt much of the recent dissatisfaction with U.S. growth is motivated by unfavorable comparisons with other countries, especially the Soviet Union. If current rates are mechanically extrapolated, it is easy to calculate that the United States will not be first in international statistical comparisons in our great-grandchildren's textbooks. Presumably the American nation could somehow stand and even rationalize this blow to our national pride, even as we survive quadrennial defeats by Russian hordes in the Olympics. At any rate, it is not for professional economists to advise the country to act differently just to win a race in statistical yearbooks. The Cold War will not be so easily won, or lost, or ended.

International competition in growth may, however, be of importance in the battle for prestige and allegiance among the "uncommitted" and less developed countries. These nations place a high premium on rapid economic progress. They will not—so the argument runs—choose the democratic way in preference to Communism, or market economies in preference to centrally directed economies, unless our institutions show by example that they can outperform rival systems. A political psychologist rather than an economist should evaluate this claim. But it has several apparent weaknesses: (a) Rate of growth is not the only dimension of economic performance by which our society will be judged by outside observers. Equality of opportunity and of condition, humanity, understanding, and generosity in relation to less privileged people in our own society and abroad—these are perhaps more important dimensions. (b) The United States is not the only non-Communist economy. The examples of Western Europe (in particular the contrast of Western to Eastern Germany) and Japan are more relevant to the rest of the world, and they give convincing evidence of the economic vitality of free societies. (c) What is much more important is a demonstration that an underdeveloped country can progress rapidly under democratic auspices. Without this kind of demonstration, faster growth of affluence in already affluent societies may cause more disaffection than admiration.

On the score of national strength, there is a case for growth. But it is more subtle than the facile association of military power with generalized civilian economic capacity. Nuclear technology has made this connection looser than ever. A country is not necessarily stronger than another just because it has a higher GNP. Great productive capacity may have been the decisive reserve of military strength in the last two world wars, but nowadays it is useless if it remains unmobilized until the cataclysmic buttons are pushed. A country with smaller GNP can be as strong or even stronger if it persistently allocates enough of its GNP to military purposes. And in the age of overkill, apparently there can be a point of saturation.

Should we grow faster to be better prepared to meet possible future needs for output for military purposes—or for other uses connected with national foreign policy? If we do not, we will have to meet such needs when they arise by depriving other claimants on national production, principally consumption, at the time. But in order to grow faster, we have to deprive these claimants now. Hence the national-power argument seems to boil down to the economist's calculation after all, i.e. to the terms of trade between current and future consumption.

But there is an important exception. Some hazards are great enough to bias our choice to favor the future over the present, to accept less favorable payoffs than we otherwise would. We might conceivably be challenged one day to a duel of overriding priority, involving all-out commitment of resources to military uses, foreign aid, space adventures, or all of these together. A high GNP might be the difference between victory and defeat rather than the difference between more or less consumption. In other words, this contingency is one that could be met only by sacrifices of consumption in advance, not by sacrifices at the time.

As for national purpose, it is surely conceivable that a growth target could inspire, galvanize, and unite the nation. But it is not the only objective that could serve this purpose, nor is it necessarily the best candidate.

Growth in What?

The formulation of the growth issue sketched above presents it as a choice among available consumption paths. The concentration on consumption deserves some elaboration and explanation—especially because growth performance and aspiration are popularly expressed in terms of gross or net national product.

Some of the noneconomic reasons for favoring faster growth also suggest that GNP is the relevant measure, especially if it is the most usual and visible measure. But as economists we would make welfare or utility depend on consumption. We would require the investment part of GNP to derive its value from the future consumption it supports. After all, a future in which the rate of growth of GNP reaches fantastic heights has no appeal if the fruits of the achievement are never consumed. We must heed the "golden rule" of capital accumulation: there is a saving ratio and a corresponding capital intensity that maximize consumption. Persistent saving in excess of the rule makes GNP higher but consumption lower.[1]

1. E. S. Phelps, "The Golden Rule of Accumulation," *American Economic Review, 51* (September 1961), 638–42.

Neither GNP nor consumption, as ordinarily measured, counts leisure. Yet I do not understand advocates of faster growth to be taking a stand in favor of goods and services priced in the market

Figure 9.2. Suggested Criterion of Intertemporal Impartiality

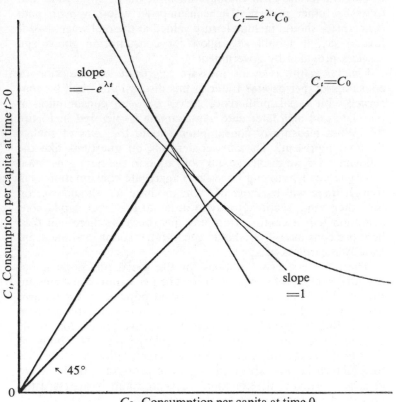

$C_t = e^{\lambda t} C_0$

slope $= -e^{\lambda t}$

$C_t = C_0$

C_t, Consumption per capita at time $t > 0$

slope $= 1$

45°

0

C_0, Consumption per capita at time 0.

and against leisure. Should the trend toward shorter hours, longer vacations, and earlier retirements accelerate, the rate of growth of consumption as measured in the national accounts might decline. But a decline for this reason should not bother a growth-oriented economist. *The Affluent Society* to the contrary notwithstanding, the conventional wisdom of economics was long since liberated from the fallacy that only produced goods and services yield utility and welfare. Economists do have prejudices against biasing the price system in favor of leisure and against forcing the leisure of involuntary unemployment on anyone. But those are other matters. The consumption whose growth path concerns us should include leisure valued at the real wage. Needless to say, it should also allow for consumption goods and services provided by government.

Finally, is the relevant measure aggregate consumption or consumption per capita? Later in this discussion I shall be concerned with social indifference curves between consumption at one date and at a later date. An example is pictured in Figure 9.2. What measure of consumption should the axes of such a diagram represent? The answer depends on questions like the following: Do we discharge our obligation to the next generation if we enable them to enjoy the same aggregate consumption even though there will be more of them to share it? Should we, on the other hand, sacrifice today in order to raise per capita consumption half a century from now just because there will then be more consumers? Or should generations count in some sense equally regardless of size?

These are not easy questions for the social philosopher, but revealed social preferences lean toward per capita consumption. Presumably we do not value increase in population for its own sake. We might if sheer numbers were important for national power. But in general we are content to leave population trends to free choice; indeed, we seek to enlarge parents' ability to limit births at their discretion. Neither immigration nor subsidies for childbearing are advanced as growth proposals. In the world at large, certainly, the commonly accepted aim is to retard the growth of population, not to accelerate it.[2]

2. T. C. Koopmans, "On the Concept of Optimal Economic Growth," Cowles Foundation Discussion Paper No. 163 (1963), presented at a joint session of the American Economic Association and the Econometric Society on "Intertemporal Economic Theory," Boston, December 1963.

Government's Power to Influence Growth

I come now to the question whether the government can influence growth, even if we wish it to. The growth objective is commonly framed in terms of an exponential growth rate. Those who advocate measures to promote growth frequently are expressing a preference for a higher per annum rate of growth, for 4 per cent or 5 per cent instead of 3 per cent or 3½ per cent. But the thrust of much recent theorizing and model building is that in the really long run we have no choice about the growth rate.[3] The long-run growth rates of GNP and aggregate consumption are exogenously determined by the growth of the labor force and the progress of technology. Or, to express the same conclusion somewhat differently, the rates of growth of productivity per man and of consumption per capita are in the long run controlled by the rate of advance of technology.

According to these models, there are various hypothetical paths which share the exogenously determined rate. These paths differ in level. On a higher path, consumption per capita is always larger than on a lower one. A higher path represents a higher capital intensity (so long as capital intensity does not exceed its golden rule value), and a correspondingly higher propensity to save is required to maintain it.

An economy moving along one of these paths may "decide" to move to a higher one, by lowering its propensity to consume. For a while, its growth rate will be higher, as the effects of increasing capital intensity and modernization are added to those of the underlying progress of technology. Eventually, however, capital intensity will cease to increase and the growth rate will converge to its natural value. The process can be repeated by further increases in the saving ratio, but the golden rule argument cited above sets a limit long before the propensity to consume reaches zero—indeed, when the propensity to save is equal to the elasticity of output with respect to capital accumulation. This is the highest path for consumption per capita.

Asymptotically, then, it appears that we have no choice about

3. E. S. Phelps, "The New View of Investment: A Neoclassical Analysis, *Quarterly Journal of Economics, 76* (November 1962), 548–67.

our rate of growth, but can choose only between parallel paths of different levels. But asymptotically is a very long time. The period of transition from one path to another, short from the perspective of the model builder, may be measured in decades or generations. It is therefore not wholly misleading to regard society as choosing among growth rates.

Models of this kind take the rate of technological progress as exogenous. In fact, it is probably subject to improvement, like the degree of capital intensity, by expenditure of current resources. We still know very little about the technology that governs the production of applicable technological knowledge. What is required to keep the index of technology, which determines the productivity of labor and capital, growing at a constant exponential rate? Does it take simply a constant absolute amount of labor and capital? Does it take a constant fraction of the resources devoted to production? Does it take an input of resources growing at the same rate as the technology index itself? Only when we can answer such questions can we know whether and how the pace of economic growth is ultimately limited by the natural increase of the labor force.

A second reason for doubting that government measures can affect the intertemporal choices of society is the possibility that the private decisions of individuals can and will offset these measures. Suppose, for example, that the government levies new taxes and uses the proceeds for saving and investment, either through public expenditure or through public lending to private investors or through retirement of public debt. The government's purpose is to increase later consumption at the expense of earlier. But if this purpose is perfectly well understood, will not the public reduce its private saving in the knowledge that its collective saving is now doing part of the job?

I have two comments regarding this possibility. First, it may be that the government's saving corrects a situation of underinvestment, where public or private projects that would pay for themselves in social benefits (discounted at the time preference set of interest rates) were not being undertaken. In this case, government's twist of the path will not be undone even if perfectly understood because the new path corresponds better to public preferences. Second, the assumption that the public correctly foresees all the consequences of government policy is farfetched. In the example above, economists would usually expect the new taxes to be paid in large part out of private consumption. Disposable income is reduced; and so, gradually, is the public's net financial claim on the government—a more tangible element in private balance sheets than the present value of future tax liabilities or of free services from government.

I conclude, therefore, that at least for the medium run, government can affect the growth of the economy; and I turn to the question whether it should.

In this section I propose to argue: (1) that government might legitimately have a growth policy, and indeed could scarcely avoid having one, even if private capital markets were perfect; (2) that capital markets are far from perfect and that private saving decisions are therefore based on an overconservative estimate of the social return to saving; and (3) that the terms on which even so advanced an economy as our own can trade present for future consumption seem to be very attractive.

Government Neutrality in Intertemporal Choice

Many economists and many other citizens will argue that the government should be neutral as between present and future. In their view the capital markets produce an optimal result, balancing the time preferences of individuals, freely expressed through their consumption and saving behavior, against the technological opportunities for substituting consumption tomorrow for consumption today. Let us assume for the moment that government can be neutral in some meaningful sense and that the capital markets perform their assigned function. Even so, I believe government should have a growth policy, and only by accident a neutral one.

I fail to see why economists should advise the public that it is wrong for them collectively to supplement (or diminish) the provisions for the future they are making individually. I agree to the desirability of satisfying human preferences—that is what our kind of society and economy is all about. But I have never been able to understand why the preferences of individuals are worthy of respect only when they are expressed in the market, why the preferences of the very same individuals expressed politically should be regarded as distortions. Sometimes economists come close to rationalizing all market results and private institutions by the argument that they would not occur and survive if they were not optimally satisfying individuals' preferences. But political results and public institutions are not granted the benefit of presumptive justification-through-existence.

In both arenas preferences certainly need to be guided by full and accurate information. In the arena of government policy, it is the business of economists to help the society know what it is doing, to understand the choices, benefits, costs, and risks it confronts, not simply to repeat *ad nauseam* that the best thing to do is nothing.

The case for explicit government policy in intertemporal social choice is especially strong. More than any other social institution, government represents the permanence and continuity of the society. And in a democracy one way in which each generation uses government is to protect the interests of unborn generations against its own shortsighted and selfish instincts.

We cannot be sure that lineal family ties will give individuals sufficient motivation to provide for society's future. Suppose the individuals of a whole generation, deciding that their children and grandchildren might better start from scratch, were to proceed to consume their capital. Good capital markets might reflect this epidemic of acute time preference in a perfectly Pareto-optimal way. But would we as a nation feel that we were collectively discharging our obligations to our successors?

Through many activities of government, including conservation and public education, we have recognized a generalized obligation to equip the next generation—an obligation wholly distinct from our individual provisions for our own children. This generalized obligation acquires special force if we take seriously our ideals of equality of opportunity. We like to think that our society gives the members of each generation an equal chance in the race, or at least that their chances are not pre-determined by family backgrounds. Besides requiring invest-ment in human beings on a basis other than ability to pay, this ideal suggests redistributive taxation of estates. And if estate taxation dulls incentives to save for specific heirs, the govern-ment needs to replenish saving collectively.

But what is growth-neutral government finance anyway? I have already dismissed as farfetched one answer; namely, that any government finance is growth neutral when it is fully and accurately foreseen, and accordingly offset, by taxpayers and by the beneficiaries of government services. Often a balanced budget is considered a growth-neutral fiscal policy. The budget in this rule is not, of course, the conventional U.S. administrative budget. Rather the rule suggests that (*a*) net government in-vestment should be covered by borrowing, with the Treasury competing in the capital markets with private investors for private saving, and that (*b*) other government expenditure, including allowance for consumption of public capital, should be covered by current taxes or fees.

The rule is clear-cut and has intuitive appeal. But it seems to bias social choice against the future when there is simply a shift in public preference from private consumption, present and future, to collective consumption, present and future. The rule would levy only enough new taxes to cover the additional collective consumption. But the evidence is that taxpayers would pay some of these new taxes from saving (especially if the collective consumption the taxes financed were of re-grettable necessities like national defense rather than of services that clearly yield utility now and in future). Interest rates would rise and investment would be curtailed, even though no shift in social time preference has occurred. Clearly the 10 per cent of GNP which the Cold War has forced us to devote per-sistently to national defense has not come wholly from private or public consumption. True neutrality evidently would require a tighter fiscal policy the bigger the government's budget for current consumption.

But in any case, the quest for neutrality is probably a search for a will-o'-the-wisp. For it is not only the overall budget posi-tion of government but also the specifics of taxation and expenditure that affect intertemporal choices. We have not yet learned how to implement the welfare economist's lump-sum taxes. I have already given one example of a tax which is desirable in view of other social objectives but is bound to affect incentives for private accumulation of wealth. It will suffice to remind you also that our methods of taxation necessarily favor one kind of current consumption, leisure, both as against other current consumption and as against future consumption of products and leisure.

The major policy proposals of growthmen boil down to the suggestion that government should save—or save more—by making investments on its own account, subsidizing the investments of others, or by channeling tax money through the capital markets into private investment. This last item is the major purpose of the full employment budget surplus for which Councils of Economic Advisers longed under both Presidents Eisenhower and Kennedy.

It is now widely recognized that in principle the government can match aggregate demand to the economy's capacity in a variety of ways. Its various instruments for regulating or stabilizing demand affect consumption and investment differently. A strong pro-growth policy would restrict consumption by taxation or by economy in government's current expenditure while stepping up public investment and encouraging private investment through tax incentives or low interest rates and high liquidity. The government cannot avoid choosing some combination of its demand-regulating instruments. Therefore government is bound to affect the composition of current output and society's provision for the future. Let us debate this choice of policy mixtures on its merits, weighing growth against its costs and against other objectives of policy, without encumbering the debate with a search for that combination which meets some elusive criterion of neutrality.

Imperfections in Private Capital Markets

I turn now to the second subject: the efficiency of the capital markets. Do private saving decisions reflect the real payoffs which nature and technology offer the economy? There are several reasons to believe that the answer is negative.

Monopoly and Restrictions of Entry. The evidence is that the rates of return required of real investment projects by U.S. business corporations are very high—typically more than 10 per cent after allowance for depreciation, obsolescence, and taxes. Rates of this magnitude are not only required *ex ante* but realized *ex post.* Why do these rates so greatly exceed the cost of borrowed funds, the earnings-to-price ratio of equity issues, and in general the rates of return available to savers?

One reason clearly is that the relevant markets are not purely competitive. A monopolistic or oligopolistic firm limits its expansion in product markets, its purchases in factor markets, and its calls on capital markets because the firm takes into account that prices and rates in these markets will turn against it. The managers seek to maintain a market valuation of the firm in excess of the replacement cost of its assets, the difference representing the capitalized value of its monopoly power, often euphemistically called good will. Restrictions and costs of entry prevent other firms from competing this difference away. Foresighted and lucky investors receive the increases in the firm's market value in the form of capital gains. But the willingness of savers to value the assets of the firm above their cost, i.e. to supply capital at a lower rate of return than the firm earns internally, is not translated into investment either by this firm or by others. One effect is to depress rates of return in more competitive sectors of the economy. But another result is to restrict total saving and investment.

Risks, Private and Social. Risks provide a second reason for the observed divergence between the rates of return satisfactory to savers and those typically required of real investment projects. Some of these are risks to the economy as well as to the owners of the business: technological hazards, uncertainties about consumer acceptance of new products, or uncertainties about the future availability and social opportunity cost of needed factors of production. Even though these are social as well as private risks, it is not clear that society should take a risk-averse position toward them and charge a risk premium against those projects entailing more uncertainties than others. Presumably society can pool such risks and realize with a very small margin of uncertainty the actuarial return on investments.

Moreover, some of the private risks are not social risks at all. Consider, for example, uncertainties about competition and market shares; if several rivals are introducing a new process or new product, the main uncertainties in the investment calculation of each are the future actions of the others. Consider, further, the high and sometimes prohibitive cost that many firms impute to external funds—apparently as insurance against loss of control to new shareowners, or, with extremely bad luck, to bondholders. If savers were offered the rates of return asked of and earned by business investments, in the form of assets that impose no more risk on the holder than is commensurate to the social risks involved, presumably they would choose to save more.

It is true, on the other hand, that some net saving is now motivated by personal contingencies that are likewise social risks of a much smaller order. But our society has created insuring institutions, both private and public, to reduce the need for over-saving to meet such contingencies. Except in the field of residential construction, it has created few similar institutions to prevent private risk-aversion from leading to underinvestment.

External Returns to Investment. Some investments yield benefits that cannot be captured by the individual or firm making the initial outlay. Research and development expenditures and outlays for training of personnel are obvious cases in point. Government policy has already recognized this fact both in tax law and in government expenditures, and it is difficult to judge whether this recognition is sufficient. Kenneth Arrow has pointed out that not only R and D but all forms of investment activity share in some degree the property that B may learn from A's doing.[4] The support that this observation gives to a general policy of encouraging investment is somewhat tempered by reflecting that the same social process of "learning by doing" can occur in production of goods and services for current consump-

4. Kenneth Arrow, "The Economic Implications of Learning by Doing," *Review of Economic Studies, 29* (June 1962), 155–73.

tion. However, experience is most important as a teacher in new situations, and innovations are likely to require investment.

In regard to investment in human capacities and talents, it is by no means clear that public outlays are yet sufficient to reap the external benefits involved, or even that the relevant capital markets are sufficiently developed to permit individuals to earn the private benefits. I recognize that calculations of the rate of return to educational outlays depend critically on how much of these outlays are charged to current consumption. As an educator and ex-student I am inclined to rate high the immediate utility-producing powers of education.

The Payoff to Social Saving

The burden of my remarks so far is that we cannot escape considering growth or, more precisely, intertemporal choice as an issue of public economic policy. We cannot assume, either, that the market settles the issue optimally or that government can be guided by some simple rules of neutrality. We must confront head-on the question whether the social payoff of faster growth in higher future consumption validates its cost in consumption foregone today. The issue that needs to be joined is typified by the contrast between Denison,[5] who estimates a very high investment requirement for a one-point increase in the medium-term growth rate (a ten-point increase in the ratio of current gross investment to GNP) and Solow,[6] who calculates a marginal investment requirement only about one fifth as high.

Fortunately the profession has now begun the task of computing rates of return on various kinds of investment, tangible and intangible. Thanks to theoretical advances in growth models and in handling the knotty problems of technological progress, vintage capital, and obsolescence, we have a better conceptual foundation for these tasks than we did only a few years ago.

5. Edward F. Denison, *The Sources of Economic Growth in the United States and the Alternatives Before Us* (Committee for Economic Development, 1962), Chapter 12.

6. R. M. Solow, "Technical Progress, Capital Formation, and Economic Growth," *American Economic Association Papers and Proceedings, 52* (May 1962), 76–86.

Phelps,[7] using the same conceptual approach as Solow,[8] has estimated the overall rate of return on tangible investment in the United States to be about 14 per cent in 1954. And even this figure seems conservative in relation to some target rates of return of large industrial corporations reported by Lanzillotti.[9]

But whatever the true rates are, they must be compared with appropriate social rates of time preference.

Consider a family of exponential balanced-growth paths sharing a common growth rate; each member of the family has a constant saving ratio, and this ratio differs from path to path. It is also true that each path is characterized by a single technological interest rate, the same for all intervals of time. The theory of the golden rule tells us that the path of highest consumption per capita at every point in time is characterized by a gross saving ratio s equal to the elasticity of output with respect to capital α (this is also the share of nonlabor income in GNP if income distribution is governed by marginal productivity). Along the golden rule path the social rate of interest is constant and equal to the rate of increase of the "effective" labor force. This in turn is equal to the natural rate of increase in the labor force plus the annual rate of improvement in labor quality due to technical progress.

If there is no technical improvement, consumption per capita remains constant over time; and along the golden-rule path a dollar of per capita consumption saved today will produce a dollar, no more and no less, in per capita consumption tomorrow. The return on aggregate saving is just enough to keep up with population growth.

This rate of return represents impartiality between generations in this sense: When consumption per capita is the same tomorrow as today, there is no time preference; a dollar of con-

7. Phelps, "The New View of Investment."

8. R. M. Solow, "Investment and Technical Progress," in K. J. Arrow, S. Karlin, and P. Suppes, eds., *Mathematical Models in the Social Sciences 1959* (Stanford, Stanford University Press, 1960), pp. 89–104.

9. Robert F. Lanzillotti, "Pricing Objectives in Large Companies," *American Economic Review, 48* (December 1958), 921–40.

sumption per capita is valued the same whenever it occurs.[10]

When there is technical progress, both the real wage and consumption per capita will advance at the annual rate at which labor quality improves, say λ. And along the golden-rule path λ will also be the per annum rate of return, in future per capita consumption, on saving today. (A dollar of saving will yield in addition enough new capital to provide for the increment of population.) That is, an increase in per capita consumption of $1.00 at time t requires sacrifice of only $\$e^{-\lambda t}$ at time zero.

It is reasonable to regard this rate of discount, too, as intertemporally impartial. Absence of time preference means that at equal consumption levels society values equally a dollar of future consumption and a dollar of present consumption. But on a path of growing per capita consumption, it is natural that a dollar of future consumption should no longer trade for current consumption at par. To take the rate of improvement in labor quality and in the real wage, λ, as the rate of time preference is to say in effect: saving is justified if and only if it earns more than future consumers will gain anyway through the inexorable progress of technology. Thus if the rate of technical progress is correctly foreseen, this principle meets a common criticism of growth; namely, that there is no reason to save for future generations when technological progress will make them better off anyway. Figure 9.2 illustrates a social indifference curve between present and future per capita consumption such that there is no time preference when the two are equal, but elsewhere a marginal rate of substitution that exceeds one in the same proportion that future consumption exceeds current consumption.

An economy saving at a constant rate s lower than α, the share of capital income in GNP, will be below its golden-rule path. Its rate of return on saving will be accordingly higher than the golden-rule rate. Indeed the present value of the stream of returns from a dollar of investment, computed at the golden-rule rate on the theory that this is an appropriate impartial discount factor free of the taint of time preference, is equal to α/s. In the United States today the ratio α/s must exceed 1.5 and may be as high as 2.

10. Koopmans, "On the Concept of Optimal Economic Growth."

For some models it is possible to compute the technological interest rate characteristic of a path with α/s greater than one; i.e. of a path below the golden-rule path. This is, in effect, what Phelps did to arrive at his estimates of the return on investment in the United States, cited above. Consider a model based on a Cobb–Douglas production function with variable factor proportions both *ex ante* and *ex post*. Let capital elasticity be α and labor elasticity $1 - \alpha$; the natural rate of increase in labor force $n;$ constant technical progress expressed as improvement in the quality of labor at rate λ; a gross saving ratio $s;$ depreciation of capital at a constant rate δ. The members of this family of growth paths share a rate of growth $n + \lambda$ in aggregate output, investment, and consumption, and a rate of growth λ in the real wage and in per capita consumption. The rate of interest characteristic of a path is different depending whether technical progress is assumed to be (*a*) disembodied and affecting all capital old or new, or (*b*) embodied in new vintage capital only. The expressions for the rate of interest in the two cases are as follows (for their derivation see Appendix):

(*a*) disembodied technical progress

$$r = \frac{\alpha}{s}(n + \lambda + \delta) - \delta$$

(*b*) embodied technical progress

$$r = \frac{\alpha}{s}(n + \lambda + \delta) - \delta + \frac{\lambda(1 - \alpha)}{s} - \frac{\lambda(1 - \alpha)}{\alpha}$$

If, for example, $n = .015$, $\lambda = .03$, $\delta = .03$, and $s = .20$, then $r = .095$ in case (*a*) and $r = .135$ in case (*b*). The difference reflects the fact, originally emphasized by Solow,[11] that additional saving moves the economy toward a higher path faster in the vintage-capital model and therefore is rewarded sooner with higher consumption.

11. Solow, "Investment and Technical Progress."

The evidence is uncertain, and there is a clear need for more refined and reliable estimates of the parameters on which the issue turns. I believe the evidence suggests that policy to accelerate growth, to move the economy to a higher path, would pay. That is, the returns to a higher saving and investment ratio would be positive, if evaluated by a reasonable set of social time preference interest rates. This seems to me the strongest reason for advocating growth policy.

APPENDIX

1. Let $I(v)$ be gross investment at time (vintage) v, and let $p(v, t)$ be its marginal productivity at time t. Then the present value of the stream of returns from investment of one dollar at time v is

$$\int_v^\infty e^v{}^{-\int_t^t r(u)\,du} p(v, t)\,dt.$$

Setting this present value equal to 1 for all v defines the series $r(u)$ of instantaneous technological interest rates.

In the models under discussion in the text calendar time does not affect $p(v, t)$, which can therefore be written as $p(t - v)$. It follows that $r(u)$ is a constant, and we may find it from:

$$(1) \qquad \int_0^\infty e^{-r(t-v)} p(t - v)\, d(t - v) = 1$$

The gross income to capital at time t, if capital of each vintage is paid its marginal product, is

$$\alpha Q(t) = \int_{-\infty}^t I(v)\, p(v, t)\, dv = \int_0^\infty I(t - v)\, p(t - v)\, d(t - v)$$

where $Q(t)$ is gross output summed over all vintages, and α is capital's share. Now if investment is growing exponentially at rate g—

the rate of growth of output—then $I(t - v) = I(t)e^{-g(t-v)}$. Therefore

$$(2) \qquad \frac{\alpha Q(t)}{I(t)} = \frac{\alpha}{s} = \int_o^\infty e^{-g(t-v)} p(t - v) \, d(t - v)$$

where s is the saving ratio, constant along the path. The right-hand side will be recognized at the present value of the stream of returns from investment when the discount factor is g rather than r. This present value exceeds 1 whenever α/s exceeds one.

2. The above argument shows that $r \gtreqqless g$ as $\alpha \gtreqqless s$. It remains to derive the explicit expressions for r given in the text.

(a) Disembodied progress:
Let $Q(v, t)$ be the output and $L(v, t)$ the labor input associated with capital made at time v.

$$(3) \qquad Q(v, t) = A(I(v)e^{-\delta(t-v)})^\alpha (L(v, t)e^{\lambda t})^{1-\alpha}$$

The marginal product of capital:

$$(4) \qquad p(v, t) = \alpha \frac{Q(v, t)}{I(v)} = A\alpha e^{-\alpha\delta(t-v)} e^{\lambda(1-\alpha)t} \left(\frac{L(v, t)}{I(v)} \right)^{1-\alpha}$$

The marginal product of labor:

$$(5) \; w(t) = (1 - \alpha) \frac{Q(v, t)}{L(v, t)} = A(1 - \alpha)e^{-\alpha\delta(t-v)} e^{\lambda(1-\alpha)t} \left(\frac{L(v, t)}{I(v)} \right)^{-\alpha}$$

$$w(t)^{-(1-\alpha)/\alpha} = A^{-(1-\alpha)/\alpha}(1 - \alpha)^{-(1-\alpha)/\alpha} e^{(1-\alpha)\delta(t-v)}$$

$$e^{-\lambda((1-\alpha)^2/\alpha)t} \left(\frac{L(v, t)}{I(v)} \right)^{1-\alpha}$$

$$p(v, t) = A^{1/\alpha}\alpha(1 - \alpha)^{+(1-\alpha)/\alpha} e^{-\delta(t-v)} e^{((1-\alpha)/\alpha)\lambda t} w(t)^{-((1-\alpha)/\alpha)}$$

Since the real wage w grows at rate λ,

$$p(v, t) = A^{1/\alpha}\alpha(1 - \alpha)^{(1-\alpha)/\alpha} e^{-\delta(t-v)} e^{(1-\alpha)/\alpha\lambda t}(w(o)e^{\lambda t})^{-((1-\alpha)\lambda\alpha)}$$
$$p(v, t) = A^{1/\alpha}\alpha(1 - \alpha)^{(1-\alpha)/\alpha} e^{-\delta(t-v)} w(o)^{-((1-\alpha)/\alpha)}$$

Thus $p(v, t)$ can be written as $p(t - v)$ and indeed

(6) $p(v, t) = p(t - v) = p(v, v)e^{-\delta(t-v)} = p(o)e^{-\delta(t-v)}$

To find r we set $\int_0^\infty e^{-r(t-v)} p(t - v) d(t - v) = 1$
Therefore

(7) $$p(o)\int_o^\infty e^{-r(t-v)}e^{-\delta(t-v)}d(t - v) = 1$$

and $r = p(o) - \delta$. From section 1 we know

$$p(o)\int_0^\infty e^{-g(t-v)}e^{-\delta(t-v)}d(t - v) = \frac{\alpha}{s}$$

(8)   Therefore $p(o) = \dfrac{\alpha}{s}(g + \delta)$

Since $g = n + \lambda$ we have

(9) $$r = \frac{\alpha}{s}(n + \lambda + \delta) - \delta$$

(b) Embodied progress:
In this case:

(10) $$Q(v, t) = A(I(v)e^{-\delta(t-v)})^\alpha(L(v, t)e^{\lambda v})^{1-\alpha}$$

By reasoning similar to (a) we obtain

(11) $p(v, t) = A^{1/\alpha}\alpha(1 - \alpha)^{(1-\alpha)/\alpha}e^{-\delta(t-v)}e^{((1-\alpha)/\alpha)\lambda v}w(t)^{-((1-\alpha)/\alpha)}$
$p(v, t) = A^{1/\alpha}\alpha(1 - \alpha)^{(1-\alpha)/\alpha}e^{(-\delta - (1-\alpha)\lambda/\alpha)(t-v)}w(o)^{-((1-\alpha)/\alpha)}$

Once again $p(v, t)$ can be written as $p(t - v)$, and

$$p(t - v) = p(o)e^{-(\delta + (1-\alpha)\lambda/\alpha)(t-v)}$$

The same procedure used in (a) gives:

(12) $$r = p(o) - \delta - \frac{(1 - \alpha)\lambda}{\alpha}$$

and

$$p(o) = \frac{\alpha}{s}\left(g + \delta + \frac{(1-\alpha)}{\alpha}\lambda\right)$$

(13)

$$= \frac{\alpha}{s}(n + \lambda + \delta) + \frac{(1-\alpha)}{s}\lambda$$

Therefore

(14) $r = \dfrac{\alpha}{s}(n + \lambda + \delta) - \delta + \left(\dfrac{1-\alpha}{s}\right)\lambda - \left(\dfrac{1-\alpha}{\alpha}\right)\lambda.$

PART III

MONETARY POLICY AND INFLATION

INTRODUCTION

The beginning of the Korean War in June 1950, and the Chinese intervention in November, led to two waves of scare buying and hoarding by American consumers and businessmen. Since they had very recently experienced the shortages and rationing of World War II, followed by the postwar price inflation, these reactions were scarcely surprising. These buying waves increased wholesale prices by 15 per cent and consumer prices by 7 per cent in the short space of six months during the second half of 1950. This inflation preceded the real draft on the nation's productive resources occasioned by the war. The big increase in defense spending did not begin until 1951. At the President's request, Congress passed legislation increasing federal taxes in 1950 and again in 1951. Nevertheless, it was doubtful that these tax increases would suffice to contain the inflationary pressures due to the war.

What other measures should the government take? Under the Defense Production Act of 1950, machinery was established requiring supplies of scarce materials to meet defense needs ahead of other demands. Congress also authorized the President to establish federal controls over prices and wages, and in January 1951— following a renewed burst of inflationary buying when the Chinese entered the war—a general freeze of wages and prices was ordered. This was only a stopgap to hold the line while administrative machinery could be assembled to control wages and prices individually, as was done by the OPA during the Second World War.

Many economists, and many other citizens, were strongly opposed to a revival of these *direct controls* over wages and prices.

In their view, the anti-inflationary job could and should be done by the *indirect controls* of fiscal and monetary policy. Since taxes were being increased substantially, probably to their political limit, attention naturally focused on monetary policy.

Anti-inflationary monetary policy had been limited, throughout the Second World War and the years following, by the Federal Reserve's wartime commitment to purchase long-term government bonds at par. This made it easy for holders of these bonds to spend them, or for lending institutions to finance increased private spending by selling their government bonds and replacing them with new and higher-yielding private loans and securities. Moreover, whenever the Federal Reserve purchased such bonds, it increased bank reserves and made possible a *multiple* expansion of bank credit.

In March 1951 the Treasury and Federal Reserve reached their now-famous "accord," which released the Federal Reserve from its commitment to support the prices of government bonds. Opponents of direct controls felt that the Federal Reserve should use its new freedom vigorously to raise interest rates, lower bond prices in the market, and restrict bank reserves and credit. They preferred general monetary restriction of this type not only to direct controls over prices and wages but also to the direct and selective controls over credit that were being adopted: regulations governing the terms of consumer credit and residential mortgages, and "voluntary" restraints on bank lending.

I sympathize with this viewpoint in peacetime situations. As other essays in this volume make clear, I believe that the indirect controls of general monetary and fiscal policy are normally adequate to prevent inflation due to excess demand. In the circumstances of the Korean War, however, I could see a place for direct controls, and the essay reprinted as Chapter 10, written in 1951, tells why.

Prices were remarkably stable during the remainder of the Korean War, 1951–53 and through the succeeding two years. The war did not escalate, and public psychology calmed down. Tax increases, moderately restrictive monetary measures, and direct controls all played some part. Another factor, to which attention is called in Chapter 11, originally written in early 1956, was the decline in agricultural prices. Earlier, as indicated in Chapter 11, economists worried whether full employment and price stability were consistent goals. It was feared that full employment might lead labor unions and other workers to seek—and employers to grant—wage increases exceeding gains in productivity. The 1951–55 experience seemed to justify optimism on this score, but Chapter 11 warned that this favorable experience might be the result of agricultural price declines that could not be expected to continue.

The subsequent boom of 1956–57 led to a resumption of cost and price inflation, and to a renewal of pessimism concerning the compatibility of full employment and price stability. Since the economy has not returned to full employment since 1957, the issue is still in doubt. Official exhortations of management and labor unions, informal Presidential interventions in steel wage negotiations and pricing decisions, the 1962 wage–price guideposts of the Council of Economic Advisers—these are all attempts to hold down costs and prices without the compulsion of wartime direct controls.

Another method, of course, is to keep overall demand so low, compared to the economy's capacity in manpower and industrial plant, that wages are restrained by the competition of unemployed workers and prices disciplined by the competition of idle capacity. This can be done by relatively tight monetary and fiscal policies. Prevention of a recurrence of the 1956–57 burst of inflation was the major preoccupation of the Federal Reserve in the years following. It was also a major goal of the fiscal and debt management policies of the Eisenhower Administration. In Chapter 6 I expressed my view that this goal was being given much too high priority.

I repeated this view, with specific reference to the Federal Reserve, in the essay reprinted as Chapter 12. This concerned possible revisions of priorities in monetary and fiscal policy that might occur under the Kennedy Administration. I wrote the essay before I had any intimation that I might serve in the Administration myself. The essay suggests that the new Administration, so far as it would influence monetary policy, might place higher priorities on full employment and on growth than its predecessor.

However, it recognized that balance-of-payments difficulties would stand in the way, unless new international monetary arrangements could be quickly negotiated. The importance of such arrangements, and their nature, are discussed in Part IV. In retrospect it is clear that, writing in 1960, I greatly underestimated the resistance to negotiating new arrangements both in the United States and in Europe. Progress toward reforms that would liberate U.S. monetary policy to serve less equivocally the domestic goals of full employment and growth has been slow. Nevertheless there has been, I believe, some reorientation of monetary policy in the directions suggested in Chapter 12.

By the spring of 1965, recovery from the 1960 recession had been proceeding uninterrupted for more than four years. This expansion had produced virtually no price increases or capacity bottlenecks. Neither had it succeeded in eliminating excessive unemployment and idle industrial capacity. Some observers therefore felt that the government should provide additional fiscal or monetary stimulus in order to reach full employment and avoid a possible recession. But the very durability of the expansion led others to fear that it would get out of hand and explode into a speculative boom. In their view the best way to prolong the expansion was to slow it down; they would have the government apply the brake, not the accelerator.

But the debate involved more than the strategy of domestic economic stabilization. There were strong pressures in 1965 for tighter monetary policy and higher interest rates in order to prevent dollars from flowing abroad. Largely because of General de Gaulle's impatience with the United States, gold losses were the largest in five years. The Administration had adopted voluntary programs to limit exports of capital by U.S. banks and business firms, but many financial observers here and abroad felt that these should be reinforced by raising U.S. interest rates.

The controversy took a dramatic turn when Chairman William McChesney Martin, Jr., of the Board of Governors of the Federal Reserve System warned, in a commencement speech at Columbia University on June 1, 1965, that the expansion of the 'sixties bears disquieting similarities to the ill-fated boom of the 'twenties. The speech was widely interpreted to mean that Chairman Martin was contemplating a tighter monetary policy. His warnings contributed to a substantial decline in the stock market. In the article reprinted as Chapter 13 I contested Chairman Martin's interpretation of history and advocated a policy to invigorate and extend the expansion of the 'sixties. I argued that the gold value of the dollar was already receiving too absolute a priority in U.S. policy.

Chapter 10

Monetary Restriction and Direct Controls

The evangelical advocacy of monetary restriction which has characterized much recent discussion of anti-inflationary policy has been coupled with an equally fervent opposition to direct controls over prices and wages. Most economists agree that taxation is the major weapon against inflation; the discussion of monetary restriction and direct controls concerns the choice of an auxiliary weapon. I shall argue that, in the present circumstances resulting from the Korean War, direct controls are a more useful adjunct to anti-inflationary fiscal policy than monetary restriction.

The question arises, of course, why fiscal policy requires any adjunct at all. Cannot taxation do the job alone? There are three reasons why it needs help:

1. Because of expectations that the worst is yet to come, the inflationary gap may continue to exceed the gap attributable to the armament program. Congress and the public may be persuaded to put up the taxes necessary to pay the costs of defense, but it is understandably difficult to convince them of the necessity for further taxes to yield a budget surplus.

2. The disincentive effects of taxation make it desirable to supplement fiscal policy by other measures.

3. The economy is threatened with two distinct species of inflation. The first kind, "gap" inflation, is generated by excess demand; increases in prices, wage rates, and money incomes are the consequence and not the cause. The second kind, "income" inflation, is generated by successful demands to raise wages and other money incomes; this may occur even in the absence of

Originally published in *Review of Economics and Statistics, 33* (August 1951), 196–98. Copyright, 1951, by the President and Fellows of Harvard College.

excess demand. Fiscal policy is an effective antidote to "gap" inflation, but it cannot prevent "income" inflation. Indeed the attempt to cure a "gap" inflation by taxation may even provoke an "income" inflation; unions may ask for higher money wages to offset tax increases just as they demand compensation for price increases. What taxation, especially progressive income taxation, *can* do is to insure that labor is punished for an inflationary wage policy. The punishment is unemployment. It will not necessarily stop the inflation, and it is costly to the whole economy. The cost, severe enough in peacetime, is intolerable in the present emergency.

Monetary restriction shares the weakness of fiscal policy in coping with "income" inflation. It too cannot prevent such an inflation but can only punish the economy for its sins. (Monetary restriction does offer less occasion than taxation for demands to boost money incomes, although tighter terms on home mortgages and consumer credit act in the same direction as higher taxes or higher prices.) Only direct controls of wages and prices can be relied upon to prevent this species of inflation.

But even if the inflationary danger were exclusively of the "gap" variety, the case for monetary policy is not clear-cut. The effectiveness of monetary restriction depends upon an unsettled empirical question: how interest-elastic are investment and consumption demands? To judge from the confidence with which the advocates of monetary policy offer their advice to the nation, either they are very sure of the answer to this question or they are willing to push interest rates to whatever heights necessary to accomplish a given curtailment of demand.

If the effectiveness of changing interest rates by 1 or 2 per cent is doubtful in peacetime, it is even more doubtful now. The reason for this is illustrated by the psychological basis of the recent inflation. On June 25, 1950, goods suddenly became a much more attractive, and liquid assets a much less attractive, means of holding wealth. To a nation so recently schooled in the economics of war, Korea foretold both inflation and the eventual rationing, official or unofficial, of civilian goods. The inflation which then beset the country was the result not of defense spending but of inventory accumulation in the widest sense. Consumers and businessmen, at every stage of the productive process, sought to build up their stocks of goods, to make the composition of their wealth correspond to their revised valuation of physical assets relative to liquid assets. (It should be noted that the same fears which produce an inflationary gap provide motivation for income demands which can set off "income" inflation.)

Monetary restriction reduces an inflationary gap in two ways: (1) by increasing the earnings of liquid assets relative to the returns, actual or imputed, from holding goods, and (2) by inflicting capital losses on the owners of liquid assets. An inflation inspired by fear of war is a formidable opponent to both attacks.

1. To a nation fearing a hot war of indefinite duration, frozen meats are a better bet than liquid assets. The yield on liquid assets must, first of all, compensate holders for the inflation which they anticipate. On the basis of the last decade of war and near-war, the public might reasonably expect inflation during the coming decade at a rate of 6 per cent per year. The yield must also offset the attractiveness that certain goods possess because of the vivid possibility that they may become unobtainable at any price for an indefinite period. If a consumer is without a new house, a new car, a television set, and a deepfreeze full of steaks when that day comes, he anticipates small consolation from the knowledge that his safe-deposit box harbors a piece of paper whose value is keeping pace with some price index. Even equities and Professor Slichter's cost-of-living savings bonds lack the advantages of durable or storable goods.

2. The "capital loss" effect of monetary restriction is very similar to the effect of inflation itself. In one case, real capital losses are inflicted on the owners of liquid assets by a fall in the market values of the assets; in the other, they are inflicted by a rise in the prices of goods. These real capital losses are the natural short-run consequence of the community's desire to shift its wealth from liquid assets to goods. In time this desire can be satisfied by adding to the stock of goods from new production. Meanwhile it can only be satisfied by increasing the value of existing goods relative to liquid assets. In the past year, Federal Reserve support of the bond market has forced this change in relative values to occur exclusively by a rise in the prices of goods. Holders of

liquid assets have suffered an 8 per cent real capital loss from inflation. A similar loss could have been inflicted upon them by a rise in interest rates; but since many liquid assets are demand or short-term obligations, the required increase in interest rates would have been very large. Moreover, private individuals are to a great extent protected from feeling such losses, until they are disastrously severe, by a network of intermediary financial institutions. The danger is that the policy would not be effective unless the losses were disastrously severe.

It may well be, therefore, that effective monetary policy would require such a large and rapid increase in interest rates that the accompanying capital losses would be almost as unpalatable to holders of liquid assets as inflation itself. This is not an argument in favor of supporting government bonds at par; as noted above, no one *knows* the interest-elasticities of investment and consumption demand—they might prove to be high. It is a warning against the impression, which the public is gaining from the vehemence with which many economists have been calling for monetary measures, that only stubborn Treasury stupidity blocked a highly certain and relatively painless cure for inflation.

If the source of inflationary pressure is, as it was in 1951, fear of war, inflation, and shortages, direct controls do not deserve scornful dimissal as treating the symptoms and not the disease. For one thing, sometimes a measure is the only effective way of dealing with the situation that anticipation of the measure itself helps to create. The devaluation of the British pound is an example. This point aside, prompt and resolute imposition of direct controls could have provided a demonstration, more convincing than the adoption of any other policy, that the inflation which everyone feared and anticipated would not be permitted to occur. This in itself would have removed much of the basic inflationary pressure. Perhaps it is not too late. So long as total war does not come, direct controls can provide a breathing period while the appetite for durable goods is satisfied from new production. There are already some signs that it is beginning to be satisfied. Under present lukewarm war plans, the buildup of military capacity and stocks at the expense of civilian demands will be concentrated in the next two years. Even during that period civilian durable goods will be produced. When the buildup period is over, controls can probably be abandoned. In the interim they can serve the useful purpose of holding the line while (1) the sudden psychological shift of 1950 is gradually reversed both by the prevention of further inflation and by the continued failure of the dreaded cataclysm to occur and (2) new production gradually satisfies the desire to shift wealth holdings to goods. Of course the war may become total before controls can be removed. In that case, surely not even the most ardent advocate of monetary measures and the price system would be unhappy to have direct controls already in force.

Chapter 11

Labor and Economic Stabilization

Experience in the second half of the 1950s has dissipated many of the fears of the first five years concerning the prospects of successful stabilization policy. The dilemma between inflation and unemployment, supposedly created by the power that full employment gives strong trade unions to enforce insatiable demands for increases in money wages, does not appear nearly so intractable in 1956 as it did in 1951. The nightmare of an economy of special-interest groups who use their economic and political power to escalate wages and prices upward in a continuous competitive scramble has given way to the American dream of an ever-growing full-employment economy with a stable, or at worst slowly rising, price level. Economists are notoriously susceptible to the current economic climate, and we should not be guilty in 1956 of dismissing too hastily the problems that seemed so formidable only five years ago. Perhaps a consideration of the reasons the United States has escaped these difficulties in recent years will contribute to an appraisal of their importance for the future.

It is certainly conceivable that demands of labor, and of other groups, for higher rates of money income can make it impossible for the government to maintain high employment without inflation. The economy does, it is true, contain certain automatic mechanisms that penalize these demands by reductions in aggregate employment and output—mechanisms that operate, at any rate, so long as a self-generating spiral of expectations of price and wage increases is not set off. These mechanisms include (1) the progressive tax structure, which collects a higher per-

Originally published in Gerhard Colm, ed., *The Employment Act, Past and Future* (Washington, National Planning Association, 1956).

centage of income at higher price levels than at lower; (2) the net liquid wealth of business firms and households, which decreases in purchasing power as prices rise; (3) the terms and availability of credit, which tighten as higher money incomes increase cash needed to handle transactions. But government officials with responsibility for economic stabilization are bound to be reluctant to permit these mechanisms to operate. The penalties of unemployment and reduced output are severe social costs; they hit the innocent and may leave the guilty unscathed and undeterred. Suspension of the mechanisms by expansionary fiscal and monetary policies evidently commits the government to ratify every upward push of money wage rates and prices and removes the price level from effective public control. A still darker picture can be painted in which the stabilization authorities have not only lost control of the price level but are even powerless to increase employment because organized labor and other groups respond to each expansionary fiscal and monetary dose by an increase in money wages and prices.

One of the numerous chicken–egg arguments in economics is whether, during an inflation, money wage increases are a cause of or a response to rises in the cost of living. With the hindsight now available, our postwar inflation looks much more like the demand-pull than the cost-push species. This same hindsight adds conviction to the arguments of Friedman and Rees that unions, far from accelerating the rate of wage increase, actually retarded it by fixing wages contractually for periods of a year or more. The backlog of demand for durable goods by households and business firms, supported by their abnormal accumulations of liquid wealth, was the primary cause of inflation; and just when this backlog began to taper off and the economy, partly by the growth of physical wealth and partly by inflation itself, grew up to its liquid wealth, Korea brought a final inflationary spurt. The inflationary gap, particularly in the markets for durable goods, gave unions abnormally great bargaining power in terms of the profit opportunities they could deny to employers by work stoppages. At the same time, rises in the cost of living provided both an ample motivation and an appealing argument for wage increases.

Table 11.1. *Average Annual Percentage Rates of Increase in*
Selected Measures of Wage Rates

	Period		
	Dec. 1945 to Dec. 1950	Dec. 1946 to Dec. 1950	Dec. 1950 to Dec. 1955*
Average Hourly Earnings (B.L.S.)			
All manufacturing	9.2	8.0	4.6
Bituminous coal	9.5	7.9	5.7
Wholesale trade	7.8	6.4	4.6
Telephone	7.3	6.2	5.0
Hotels (year-round)	7.8	5.3	4.6
Other Measures			
Class I Railways, average	10.6	8.7	4.0
Construction, common labor, E.N.R.	10.9	9.7	5.9
Construction, skilled labor, E.N.R.	9.0	8.4	5.0

*December 1955 estimated from latest monthly average available, November, October, or September.

The virtual stability of the cost of living during the second half of the first postwar decade can be explained in only small part by slackening in the rate of increase of money wages relative to productivity. Money wage rates have not risen as fast as during the first half; but if the headlines have been less full of spectacular "rounds" of wage increases won by major unions, there has been a steady rise in the pay of smaller unions and unorganized workers, some of whom fell behind during the previous inflation. The average productivity of manufacturing labor has risen somewhat more slowly since 1950; the productivity of the nonagricultural labor force in general has risen at about the same rate. The dramatic change in the supplies and prices of agricultural products is the main factor in the differential history of the consumer price index and of the real wage rate during the two periods. The food and apparel components of the index rose sharply until 1951 and have since leveled off. The rest of the index has been rising at a rate that shows little diminution between the earlier and later halves of the decade. Evidently the rise in money wages since 1950 was too fast to be absorbed entirely by the advance in productivity. But the resulting industrial price increases were offset by declines in agricultural prices. Without this safety valve, the earlier fears that full employment plus trade unions must explode into inflation might well have been justified. Especially if the farmers are successful in mobilizing their economic and political strength, this safety valve will not always exist.

Table 11.2. Selected Indicators of Changes in Productivity
(Average Annual Percentage Increase)

	1946–1950 (four years)	1950–1954 (four years)	1950–1955 (five years)
I. Manufacturing Productivity[a]	6.2	....	3.3
II. Nonagricultural Productivity[b]	1.6	1.6	....

a. A/BC where A is F.R.B. manufacturing production index, annual average, B is number of production and related workers in manufacturing, B.L.S., annual average, C is average weekly hours of work in manufacturing, B.L.S., annual average. 1955 data are eleven-month averages.

b. A/B where A is Commerce Department gross private nonfarm product in constant dollars, B is civilian nonagricultural employment, Census, annual average. 1955 figures were unavailable, and 1954 was used instead.

If not, the compatibility of high employment and price stability will depend in great part on the economic and political strength of organized labor. In recent years, this strength seems to have been ebbing. Naturally the elimination of excess demand, especially of the backlog demand for durable goods, has meant the disappearance of some of labor's earlier bargaining power. But that is not all. Public opinion and governmental power reacted strongly, even during a Democratic national administration, when unions in essential industries tried to use their theoretical power to cripple the national economy. This reaction has removed a potent weapon from the labor arsenal. Taft–Hartley and "right-to-work" legislation in the states have operated in the same direction. Perhaps more important than the substantive provisions of these laws has been the state of public opinion of which they are symptomatic. Labor has been notably unsuccessful in mobilizing support for its campaigns against them. In this climate, restraint in the exercise of power may well appear to be the better part of valor, lest even more severe legislative restrictions be enacted. Meanwhile, diminishing returns have set in with respect to the extension of organized labor's share of the labor force.

In recent years some union leaders have been resourceful and imaginative in shifting the focus of negotiation from cash wages to deferred and contingent claims on the employer, notably retirement and unemployment benefits. This shift does not eliminate but may reduce the upward push that increases in labor costs give to the price level. To the employer, these obligations are as much a deterrent to employment of a new man as straight wages. But when the agreement is made, the employer undertakes obligations to his existing employees which are in effect fixed costs and cannot be avoided by reducing the employment he offers. The employer does not, therefore, require in order to maintain employment the same price increase that would be needed in case of a straight wage rise. These schemes probably also effect a general reduction in the propensity to consume, so that wage increases in this form strengthen the mechanisms working toward reduction in employment and output. But, as we have already noted, a government committed to high employment will offset these mechanisms anyway.

The ability of the economy to absorb money wage increases without inflation will depend on the rate of increase in labor productivity. Here the decisive factor is doubtless the march of science and technology; the importance of labor attitudes and policies can easily be exaggerated. Labor leadership increasingly recognizes that opposition to technological change may purchase temporary apparent security at the cost of ultimate disaster. But the conquest of unemployment has not turned out to be as sovereign a cure for social ills as once was hoped; war, juvenile delinquency, monopoly, tariffs, and restrictive union practices have more complicated and enduring causes. Labor's efforts to increase the security of the individual worker in a particular job have continued unabated by the general availability of jobs. So far, at least, this objective greatly overshadows the objective of moving a displaced worker to another job at a minimum of personal sacrifice. Seniority rules, make-work requirements, work standards, jurisdictional rules, etc., still interpose obstacles to increases in productivity by rationalization and technological advance in individual plants. Moreover, recent innovations in union contracts will impair somewhat the efficiency and adaptability of the economy as a whole in the future. These are provisions which, like seniority, reduce the mobility of labor: unvested rights to pensions and unemployment compensation. Previously labor relied on its political power to obtain general public provisions for these needs, provisions that did not inhibit changes of jobs. But with the decline of its political power in federal and state governments, organized labor has shifted these problems to the agenda of collective bargaining. This is a case where centralized government action is more favorable to the mobility required for the functioning of a market economy than decentralized private agreements. The problem of adjustment to technological progress is another case where bargains with individual firms or even industries cannot begin to provide an adequate solution.

On the record of the 1945–55 decade, we can hope that full employment and reasonable stability of the price level can both be achieved in a free economy. But we certainly cannot be confident. The cruel dilemma between inflation and unemployment may more or less chronically confront our stabilization efforts. The last five years may turn out to be only a temporary respite, purchased at the cost of agricultural discontent. Our main hope is in a rapid enough rate of technological advance to satisfy the aspirations of labor for continuing improvements in standards of living and in security of individual incomes. The prospects for rapid growth in productivity depend, in part, on satisfying the drive for income security by arrangements consistent with the mobility and adaptability needed in a progressive economy. So far all too little of the resourcefulness, imagination, and statesmanship of labor, industry, and government have been devoted to the objective of devising such arrangements.

Chapter 12

The Future of the Fed

Power and responsibility for economic policy in the United States are divided among the President, the Congress and the independent Federal Reserve System, the nation's central bank and monetary authority. The Kennedy Administration may find itself in sharp conflict with the Federal Reserve, even to the point where Congress must choose sides. The possible lines of conflict are plain enough to see.

A modern government must have an economic policy—a strategy for dealing with the business cycle, the balance of payments, the level of employment and output, and most recently, the rate of economic growth. Indeed, a political party is judged by the electorate on the performance of the economy during its tenure of office.

Monetary control is a major ingredient in any coherent strategy of national economic management. Western parliamentary democracies have therefore absorbed their central banks into the executive or at least made them responsible to the government. In the United States, however, the problem of defining the status of the central bank has not been solved.

This problem could not have been anticipated by the founders of the Federal Reserve System. Their innovation—which was an advance over England and other countries in 1914—was to place the regulation of the currency in a clearly governmental agency, a system of public central banks. At that time it was not necessary to spell out the relations of the Federal Reserve to the other organs of government concerned with economic policy.

In 1933 the federal government began to assume responsibility for the general economic health of the country. From then until

Originally published in *Challenge,* January 1961, pp. 24–28.

1946 the economic circumstances of depression and war obviously compelled monetary policies consistent with the major economic objectives and strategies of the Executive.

The question of the independence of the Federal Reserve arose between 1946 and 1951. During this period the Federal Reserve became convinced that restraint of inflationary demand by monetary means—the time-honored function of the central bank in defending the value of the currency—was impossible unless the Treasury changed its low interest-rate policy.

The Treasury–Federal Reserve Accord of 1951 freed the Federal Reserve from any obligation to support Treasury issues at par. The Fed's victory was important, but it could scarcely have been achieved without strong Congressional help. Economic policy is made in Congress as well as in the White House, and in 1951 that fact gained the Federal Reserve independence of Executive domination.

Since 1953 the Board of Governors of the Federal Reserve and the Administration have been in uncoerced and enthusiastic agreement on the broad lines of policy. Between them no issues of independence, authority, and responsibility have arisen.

On the other hand, the Joint Economic Committee of Congress, which did so much to rescue the Federal Reserve from President Truman and Secretary of the Treasury Snyder, has become increasingly critical of the way the Board has used its freedom. The Committee majority tried without success to push the Federal Reserve and the Administration toward less restrictive monetary policies in the interests of speeding economic expansion and lowering the costs of servicing the national debt.

Once again the "independence" of the Federal Reserve became a heated issue, a symbol of irresponsible power to some, and to others the last citadel protecting the dollar and the country from disaster. But this time the issue was independence from Congressional pressure rather than from the Executive. Under the Kennedy Administration the Federal Reserve may, for the first time, face opposition both in Congress and in the White House and Treasury.

Contrary to the impression sometimes conveyed by frantic financial editorialists, the Federal Reserve System is not a fourth branch of government. Even the Supreme Court is said to read the election returns, and the Fed cannot begin to claim the independence of the judiciary. As a distinguished and sympathetic servant and historian of the Federal Reserve, E. A. Goldenweiser, has said, "When the Board was created and organized, it was frequently referred to as the Supreme Court of Finance. Nothing could be less appropriate than this designation. The Board is not supreme, but subordinate to Congress and in some respects to the Administration."

The Board of Governors of the Federal Reserve System consists of seven governors, one appointed by the President every two years for a term of 14 years. From these seven the President appoints a chairman for a term of four years. This term does not coincide with the Presidential term; evidently from accident rather than design, it begins almost two years earlier. The chairman, however, traditionally offers a new President his resignation as chairman.

Even if William McChesney Martin resigns as chairman, and President Kennedy accepts his resignation, the new President will have to select his successor from the membership of the present Board. Not until 1962 will the President make a scheduled new appointment to the Board. These circumstances effectively prevent the President from controlling a Board that is unwilling to follow his leadership.

But, faced with a Board that does not cooperate with the general economic policy of his Administration, the President can ask the aid of Congress. The Federal Reserve is a creation of Congress. Congress could direct the Board to coordinate its policies with those of the President; Congress could establish a coordinating committee for economic policy similar to the National Security Council. Congress might, as in 1935, reconsider the whole constitution of the System.

The present Board of Governors may prefer to acquiesce in de facto arrangements for the coordination of economic policy under presidential direction, rather than to force the President and Congress to spell out these arrangements in formal legislation. Or will the present leadership of the Federal Reserve stand fast on what they regard as essential principles of political economy, hoping that conservatives of both parties in Congress and public opinion will sustain them?

The new Administration and the old Board of Governors may find themselves at odds on three interrelated strategic issues of economic policy.

The first is the proper target of price stabilization policy. Should monetary and fiscal policy aim at an unemployment rate of 3 per cent, or of 5 per cent, or at whatever level of unemployment is consistent with price stability?

The second issue concerns the roles assigned to monetary instruments, fiscal measures and direct controls in achieving price stabilization. For example, how much of the job of restraining aggregate demand should be assumed by high interest rates and tight credit, and how much by high taxes and a budgetary surplus?

The third issue is the strategy of debt management. To what extent is minimization of the Treasury's outlays for interest on the national debt a legitimate consideration in monetary policy and debt management?

Consider first the question of unemployment. Since 1953 the unemployment rate has averaged over 5 per cent. This is not because the Administration and the Federal Reserve lacked the knowledge and power to make the average less. The record reflects, instead, a conscious choice of policy. The monetary brakes were applied when unemployment tended to fall below 5 per cent; they were only slowly released even when unemployment stood at more than 5 per cent.

Neither the Federal Reserve nor the Eisenhower Administration liked unemployment for its own sake, but they liked inflation even less. In order to retard the upward creep of the price level, they kept aggregate demand from expanding enough to achieve higher levels of employment and production.

In spite of these efforts, the price level crept upward at a rate of about 1½ per cent per year. The authors of the policy were probably right in their conviction that prices would have risen still faster if aggregate demand had been held under less restraint. Unemployment and slackness of demand are defenses against wage and price increases; to operate the economy at a higher proportion of its capacity is to weaken these defenses.

This choice—between higher employment, greater production, and faster inflation on the one hand, and more unemployment, greater unutilized capacity, and a slower rate of price increase on the other—is a cruel one. No one knows the terms of the choice. If, on the average, 5 per cent unemployment is associated with a 1½ per cent per annum rate of price increase, does this mean that 4 per cent unemployment is to be associated with an annual inflation of 2, or 4 or 10 per cent per year?

We have no relevant experience from which to judge. Over the period 1947–53, unemployment averaged about 4 per cent, and the Consumer Price Index increased at an average annual rate of slightly over 3 per cent. But most of the price advance occurred in 1947, as a reaction to wartime excess liquidity and price controls, and in 1950 as a result of the panic buying triggered by the Korean War.

Is additional employment and production worth a faster inflationary creep? A 3 or 4 per cent unemployment policy would mean not only more jobs; it would also add $15 billion to $25 billion per year to national production. Is that worth a step-up in the rate of price increase to 3 per cent, 5 per cent, or 10 per cent? Clearly the answer may vary, depending on the terms of the choice. But whatever these terms are, the answer is necessarily a value judgment—which involves weighing the advantages of employment and output against the advantages of price stability.

Reasonable men of good intentions can and do differ both on what the terms of the choice actually are and on the values that should guide the choice. There is no uniquely "correct" target of economic stabilization policy, and it is an illusion to believe that there is. The Federal Reserve, supported by the Eisenhower Administration, had one view. The Democratic majority of the Joint Economic Committee felt that the sights were set at too low a level of employment and production. The President-elect has associated himself with this criticism.

Neither side is right, and neither is wrong. This is not simply a technical matter. The choice is inevitably and properly a political one. Administrations are judged, votes are sought—and won and lost—according to the economic performance of the nation as measured by the record of employment, production, and prices.

A new government has the right and the duty to make and to carry out its own judgment on the strategic and difficult choice between "fuller" employment and slower inflation.

The Federal Reserve has tended to take the view that decisions on monetary control are technical rather than political, that there is a single correct monetary policy—namely the course which, within the limits of human error, the Fed pursues. Federal Reserve spokesmen contend that the inevitable consequence of a deviation from their course of monetary restraint would be an eventual collapse which would more than offset temporary gains in employment and output.

The economic logic of this prediction is, to say the least, obscure; to most analysts it seems that it would come true only if the Fed itself lost nerve and slammed on the brakes too hard when attempting to slow down inflation. Whatever its logic, it is expounded and believed with ideological fervor inside and outside the Federal Reserve System.

This conviction may lead the Board of Governors to resist and to frustrate any effort by the Kennedy Administration to gear the federal budget and other instruments of economic policy to higher levels of employment and production.

The second possible conflict concerns economic growth. The Kennedy Administration comes to office committed to accelerating the nation's economic growth. The basic requirement of a growth policy is a shift in the composition of national output, so that a larger proportion goes into uses that enlarge future productive capacity—private and public investment, education and research. The other side of this coin is that personal consumption must take a smaller share of the national product.

The federal government can engineer such a shift by following a relatively "easy" monetary policy—using low interest rates and abundant credit to encourage investment by business firms and by state and local governments—while, at the same time, pursuing a tight fiscal policy which restrains consumer demand through taxes on incomes and consumption. The heavy reliance placed on monetary restraint over the past eight years is one of the reasons that, relative to GNP, consumption has grown while investment has fallen.

The objective should be to combine tighter fiscal controls and easier monetary policies in the right proportions, so that overall demand is just enough to keep the economy at the desired level of employment—for instance, at 3 per cent unemployment. The right combination would meet both the employment and the growth objectives of the government.

A policy of this kind does not imply inflexibly "easy" money —a rigid pattern of low interest rates such as hampered government stabilization policy from 1946 to 1951. Monetary control would still have to assume the main burden of anticipating and offsetting the week-to-week, month-to-month swings in aggregate demand. Interest rates and the availability of credit would still fluctuate, but, on the average, interest rates would be lower, and credit would be more plentiful. At the peak of a boom, a greater share of the task of preventing excess inflationary demand would be assumed by taxation and fiscal surplus.

Would the Federal Reserve accept a somewhat lesser role in the battle against inflation on the understanding that fiscal restraint would assume a larger role? Pronouncements by the Federal Reserve give little recognition to the fact that monetary policy and fiscal policy are, at least within broad limits, substitutes rather than complements. The Federal Reserve has carefully nurtured the impression that tight money is a *necessary* requirement of anti-inflationary policy and that a balanced budget or a large budgetary surplus is, too.

The Federal Reserve appears to believe that the same uniquely correct policy that is best for employment and price stability is also best for growth. A different policy might lead to faster growth for a time, but, according to Chairman Martin, "Efforts to maintain an artificial level of interest rates, either too high or too low, can only lead to cumulative financial disequilibrium, first distorting and then disrupting healthy economic growth."

Maintenance of a stable value of the dollar is, in Martin's view, the greatest contribution the central bank can make to economic growth. He has said, "It is only in an environment of confidence in such stability that savings will accumulate and credit will flow in an orderly way and in expanding volume." Like some other positions of the Board, this proposition relies more on a general faith that virtue pays than on careful empirical and theoretical analysis.

A growth-oriented policy might also call for direct controls to prevent easy money from expanding consumer credit. The Federal Reserve has administered selective controls of consumer credit during three periods in the past: 1941–47, 1948–49, and 1950–51. But the Board has increasingly taken an ideological position against selective controls, arguing that they are neither necessary nor appropriate instruments in a free peacetime economy.

The third possible source of conflict between the new Administration and the Fed concerns debt management and interest costs. From 1946 to 1951 all possibility of economic stabilization through monetary control was sacrificed to the objectives of minimizing Treasury interest outlays and protecting government bondholders against depreciation. These objectives had wholly undeserved priority in the scale of values of President Truman and Secretary of the Treasury Snyder.

The reaction to this Babylonian captivity of the Federal Reserve has been extreme, especially since 1953, when a new team sympathetic to the Federal Reserve took over the Treasury. In the Truman–Snyder era the effort to keep monetary control and debt management cheap destroyed their effectiveness. In the era of Eisenhower, Martin, Humphrey, and Anderson, the operative belief has been, or often seemed to be, that monetary control and debt management cannot be effective unless they are expensive, and the more costly the more effective.

In the Truman–Snyder period the Federal Reserve subordinated all other considerations to assuring the Treasury a ready market for its securities at the established low rates. In the Eisenhower Administration the belief that the Treasury must pay market interest rates with no help from the Federal Reserve has been carried so far that the federal government denies itself underwriting services that no private borrower would do without.

Economizing on federal debt interest charges is not a terribly important policy objective. It does not rank in the same class with growth, full employment, and inflation control. After all, interest outlays are internal transfers, from taxpayers to bondholders, and involve no draft on the productive resources of the nation. Nevertheless, such transfers involve inefficiencies and inequities, and the $3.5 billion increase in interest outlays since 1952 is not a trivial item in the federal budget. Surely it is reasonable to expect federal officials to keep interest costs down when they can do so without compromising other important objectives.

The Federal Reserve and the Humphrey–Anderson Treasury have practiced and advocated policies that add to the taxpayers' costs without adding to the efficacy of monetary policy and debt management for economic stabilization.

Two important examples will make the point. The first is Federal Reserve policy concerning reserve requirements. Reduction of bank reserve requirements is one way of giving the economy a monetary stimulus. Alternative ways are open-market purchase of government securities and reduction of the Federal Reserve discount rate.

Reduction of reserve requirements is the more expensive way, from the Treasury's point of view. Reserve requirements in effect compel banks to lend to the federal government at zero interest. When reserve requirements are reduced, more of the federal debt has to be placed at interest. Since 1951, whenever the economy has clearly needed monetary stimulus, requirements have been lowered. But when monetary restraint was called for, the Fed has sold securities instead of raising reserve requirements.

The second example is management of the maturity structure of the debt. The Treasury, seconded by the Federal Reserve, has favored contracyclical variation of the maturity structure, issuing long-term obligations in place of more liquid short-term ones to fight inflation, and also issuing shorts in place of longs to combat recession.

As the Joint Economic Committee pointed out, this can be an expensive policy to the government; borrowing long in boom times saddles the Treasury with peak interest rates for years to come. The Committee asked that the Treasury, instead, borrow long when interest rates are low (in recessions) and confine itself to short issues when interest rates are high (in boom times), leaving economic stabilization to the Federal Reserve. The Committee is correct that there are normally enough degrees of freedom in monetary control and debt management so that economy of interest cost can be sought without sacrificing stabilization objectives.

The most efficient and rational organization of federal debt operations would be to concentrate them in the Federal Reserve, giving the Fed a mandate to seek, through security operations and its other instruments, as much economy of interest outlays to the government as is consistent with the task of monetary stabilization.

The balance-of-payments deficit and the gold outflow cast long shadows over the domestic economic program of the incoming Administration. The dollar crisis has evoked, from those who support the monetary and employment policies of 1953–60, the claim that events now prove these policies to be indispensable. But the dollar has come to its present pass under those very policies, administered by a conservative Administration and an independent central bank, both dedicated above all to sound finance.

The solution lies in the sphere of international monetary agreements and mechanics rather than in the domestic domains of the Federal Reserve and the Treasury. To achieve it is the first economic task of the new Administration. Otherwise we shall not be free to follow the conservative monetary and economic policies of the 1950s, much less to embark on new domestic economic programs.

After the United States regains the freedom of action that the richest and most productive nation in the world should and must have, the question of the role of the Federal Reserve in the making and execution of national economic policy will be sharper and clearer. The wisdom, experience and technical resources of the Federal Reserve are needed in the formulation and execution of a coherent economic policy, no less for a liberal government than for a conservative regime. It will be better for all concerned if the Federal Reserve Board, the Administration, and the Congress can make a pragmatic adjustment to accommodate monetary policy to the general economic program of the government than if a bitter legislative battle must be joined over formal proposals to redefine the status of the Federal Reserve.

Chapter 13

Lessons of Monetary History

Commencements this year give high government officials both honorary degrees and rostrums from which to answer their critics. William McChesney Martin, Jr., Chairman of the Federal Reserve System since 1951, has suffered professorial attacks longer and more patiently than most officials. On June 1 he counterattacked at Columbia.

Chairman Martin named no names, and his targets were not wholly academic. They included General de Gaulle (for his mercantilistic appetite for monetary reserves, especially gold) and M. Jacques Rueff (for wanting to raise the price of gold and to make gold metal the only means of payment between governments), as well as Professor Robert Triffin (for seeking a supranational central bank).

But his main message—somewhat veiled but well enough understood in Wall Street—was that the country may need, soon if not now, tighter money and higher interest rates to protect its domestic economic health and its balance of payments. Here Chairman Martin takes issue with a host of critics, mainly academics, some of whom may even have infiltrated Washington. Many think that the current expansion needs further stimulus rather than sterner discipline and that the dollar's prestige abroad already receives too high a priority in United States policy.

Chairman Martin reads the critics lessons from the history of the 'twenties and the Great Depression. The irony is that before 1933 Chairman Martin's intellectual and official precursors were

Originally published as "What Is the Lesson of 1929?," *The New Republic* (June 19, 1965), pp. 11–12.

firmly in the saddle here and in Europe. Unlike Chairman Martin, they did not have to accommodate or even answer heretical financial views. The mistakes they made were all their own.

A boom is a trying period for a central banker who believes, like Chairman Martin, that recessions and depressions are inescapable retribution for the "maladjustments" of prosperity. Should he let such "excesses" develop? Or should he administer a dose of tight money? This medicine itself may turn prosperity into recession. But the doctor will always assure his perplexed and involuntary patients that they needed it to forestall much worse suffering later.

The current U.S. expansion is especially trying. It has been proceeding for 52 months without the degree of monetary discipline the Federal Reserve became accustomed to administer in the 'fifties. Yet it is hard even for the hypersensitive antennae of the central bank to detect any maladjustments or excesses. Since February 1961 a $150 billion expansion in total annual public and private spending has reduced unemployment from 7 to 4½ per cent, without noticeably raising prices. In the spring of 1961 Chairman Martin told Congress that unemployment was structural, i.e. that it could not be reduced by more spending except at serious risk of bottlenecks and inflation. Similar warnings, similarly unfounded, have been repeated in orthodox financial circles at every step of the recovery. Had they been heeded, the country would have lost millions of jobs and tens of billions of dollars in production and income.

Chairman Martin views economic expansion as a potentially explosive chain reaction, which only the tightest control prevents from running away. Some booms may merit this metaphor. But the current one seems in more danger of ending with a whimper than with a bang. To keep it going has required a succession of carefully timed and gauged stimuli—increases in federal spending, income tax cuts, and now excise reductions. "Leaning against the wind," the traditionally favorite posture of the Federal Reserve, is not an appropriate stance when the problem is to keep the wind blowing.

What is the lesson of 1929? Chairman Martin says: "To a large extent the disaster of 1929–33 was a consequence of maladjustments born of the boom of the 'twenties." More likely, the expansion of the 'twenties—noninflationary like the present expansion —simply ran out of steam. Instead of taking action to prolong it, Chairman Martin's predecessors tightened credit and raised interest rates. Like many contemporary observers and historians, they paid too much attention to a sideshow, stock market speculation, and too little to the main ring, the real economy.

Certainly no maladjustments or overindulgences occurred in the 'twenties that preordained that a routine recession in 1929–30 should become a worldwide economic and political catastrophe. That took incredible sins of omission and commission, all justified in the name of fiscal and financial orthodoxy. In the monetary area, the worst overt sins were *raising* the discount rate in September–October 1931 (Chairman Martin agrees this was a mistake) and in February 1933. On both occasions, the Federal Reserve's purpose was to protect the international gold value of the dollar. Chairman Martin was telling history upside down at Columbia when he blamed the severity of the depression on *in*sufficient concern for the external status of the dollar. Recovery did not begin in the United States until Roosevelt gave recovery higher priority than the gold standard.

It is true that the position of the dollar as an international reserve currency today is analogous to the role of the pound sterling from 1925 to 1931. But the lesson of the analogy is the opposite of the one Chairman Martin draws. In 1925, through an excess of orthodox zeal and a Colonel Blimp conception of imperial prestige, Britain returned to the gold standard at the 1914 parity of sterling with gold and the dollar. This made British exports too expensive. The result, foreseen by J. M. Keynes, was unemployment, civil strife, and depression. Nor did the sacrifices imposed on the British people and their trading partners overseas save for long the gold value of the pound or London's financial prestige. Britain was forced to devalue in 1931, and then British recovery began.

Chairman Martin deplores the ensuing destruction of the international gold standard. But this was the result of the Depression, not its cause. And the Depression itself owed much of its severity to the British government's previous determination to give the prestige of the pound sterling absolute priority over domestic prosperity.

It is worth noting in passing that then as now France had a "strong" currency because of previous devaluations, that then as now French threats to take gold forced deflationary policies on the United States and Britain, and that then as now France took gold anyway.

This is the history to which Chairman Martin appeals in asking us to place the international "value and status of the dollar" above all other considerations of economic policy. He excoriates "some Keynesian and neoclassical economists" for wishing the United States to follow the British 1931 example. But the issue is not really devaluation. The exchange value of the dollar in the 'sixties is by no means as unrealistically high as that of the pound in the late 'twenties. The issue is whether the maintenance of gold–dollar convertibility at the present rate has an absolute priority over all other objectives of U.S. domestic and foreign policy. Is "going off gold" such an ultimate catastrophe, like nuclear war, that we must avoid at all costs the slightest risk of its occurrence? And if, as Chairman Martin dubiously argues, the result would be worldwide depression, should we not expect more cooperation and forbearance from our allies than we are likely to receive so long as we define the problem, as he does, as a strictly American responsibility?

Both America and the world have more to gain from steady economic progress and sustained full employment in the United States than from timid obsession with foreign confidence in the dollar. Gratifying as it is, our long economic expansion has not yet restored full employment. The social costs of a persistent shortage of jobs can be observed daily in the streets of our cities and in the demoralization of those groups, notably Negroes and teenagers, who get jobs only when labor markets are tight. In a real sense these people—and the mayors, social workers, police, and antipoverty warriors who must struggle with their problems —are the victims of the shortcomings of national fiscal and monetary policy.

The identification of prosperity with imprudent self-indulgence may have an appealing Puritan ring. But it is wholly a vicarious

Puritanism, like the austerity of the international financiers who in 1931 forced the Labor government to cut the dole of the unemployed and the salaries of teachers in a vain attempt to "save" the pound. It would be criminal folly to endanger our current economic growth either by an attack on conjectural maladjustments and imagined excesses or by subservience to gold-hungry foreign central banks. As Chairman Martin said, "If monetary history were to repeat itself, it would be nobody's fault but our own."

PART IV

THE INTERNATIONAL MONETARY SYSTEM

Introduction

For a quarter of a century, from 1934 to 1959, the balance of payments and the international monetary system were of little concern to Americans. The value and acceptability of the dollar all over the world could be taken for granted.

Since 1959, however, the standing of the dollar has been threatened. No economic task has more continuously worried and preoccupied the United States government than preserving the "confidence" of world financial circles, official and unofficial, in U.S. currency.

To what extent should this objective take precedence over other goals of U.S. domestic and foreign policy—full employment, growth, development assistance, freer world trade? What are the responsibilities of deficit and surplus countries, respectively, for correcting imbalances in international payments? Do the recent difficulties of the dollar indicate that the whole international monetary system, based on gold and dollars, needs reform?

These are the questions considered in Part IV. The same questions have underlain negotiations between governments since 1960. These negotiations have taken a variety of forms: bilateral arrangements; discussions in the central bankers' "club" at the Bank of International Settlements in Basel; periodic meetings of Working Party III of the Organization for Economic Cooperation and Development; studies at ministerial and technical levels by the "Group of Ten," the major monetary powers; studies and debates in the International Monetary Fund.

At first the official line of treasuries and central banks, including our own, was to deny the need for any major reform of the international monetary system. Gradually, however, the need for reform has been officially acknowledged, and the discussions have shifted from whether to how. General de Gaulle threw something of a bombshell into the discussion early in 1965, when he announced that France was fed up with the use of dollars as international reserves and was indeed going to convert lots of them into gold. His outburst was thought to reflect in part the views of M. Jacques Rueff, who advocates establishing a gold standard with a doubled price of gold. However, the French government has proposed the replacement of dollars with a new international money, the Collective Reserve Unit or CRU, created by the major monetary powers for circulation among their central banks.

The United States has so far declined to consider seriously any proposal that would dethrone either gold or dollars as international reserves and insists that any new supplementary reserve assets be created in the International Monetary Fund rather than in any smaller group of nations. These disagreements are discussed and appraised in Chapter 17. How they will be resolved in the world monetary conference which Secretary of the Treasury Fowler proposed in July 1965 remains to be seen.

My own interest in the subject stems from my service on the Council of Economic Advisers during 1961–62, where international finance was part of my assignment. At a meeting in the Treasury on U.S. international monetary policy, my old friend and teacher Seymour Harris said, "What's Tobin doing here? He never took a course in international economics in his life." Nevertheless, I developed some definite opinions.

Chapter 14

Europe and the Dollar

The dollar crisis will no doubt be surmounted. "The dollar" will be saved. Its parity will be successfully maintained, and the world will be spared that ultimate and unmentionable calamity whose consequences are the more dreaded for never being described. The world monetary system will stay afloat, and its captains on both sides of the Atlantic will congratulate themselves on their seamanship in weathering the storm.

But the storm is in good part their own making. And if the financial ship has weathered it, it has done so only by jettisoning much of the valuable cargo it was supposed to deliver. Currency parities have been maintained, but full employment has not been. The economic growth of half the advanced non-Communist world has been hobbled, to the detriment of world trade in general and the exports of the developing countries in particular. Currencies have become technically more convertible, but important and probably irreversible restrictions and discriminations on trade and capital movements have been introduced. Some government transactions of the highest priority for the foreign policy of the United States and the West have been curtailed. Others have been "tied" to a degree that impairs their efficiency and gives aid and comfort to the bizarre principle that practices that are disreputably illiberal when applied to private international transactions are acceptable when government money is involved.

These are the costs. Were, and are, all these hardships necessary? To what end have they been incurred?

They have been incurred in order to slow down and end the accumulations of dollar obligations in the hands of European

Originally published in *Review of Economics and Statistics, 46* (May 1964), 123–26. Copyright, 1964, by the President and Fellows of Harvard College.

central banks. It is fair to ask, therefore, whether these accumulations necessarily involved risks and costs serious enough for the countries concerned and for the world at large to justify the heavy costs of stopping them.

Which is easier? Which is less disruptive and less costly, now and in the long run? To stop the private or public transactions that lead one central bank to acquire another's currency? Or to compensate these transactions by official lending in the opposite direction? I do not suggest that the answer is always in favor of compensatory finance. But the issue always needs to be faced, and especially in the present case.

Several courses were open to European countries whose central banks had to purchase dollars in their exchange markets in recent years. (1) They could have built up their dollar holdings quietly and gladly, as they did before 1959. (2) By exercising their right to buy gold at the U.S. Treasury, they could have forced devaluation of the dollar or suspension of gold payments. (3) They could have taken various measures to correct and reverse chronic European payments surpluses. (4) By occasional withdrawals of gold and by constant complaints they could bring tremendous pressure for "discipline" upon the United States without forcing a change in the dollar parity.

European central banks and governments chose the fourth course, with token admixtures of the third. They have made world opinion, and American opinion, believe there is no other choice. Almost everyone agrees that the pressure of the balance-of-payments deficit upon the United States is inescapable arithmetic rather than the deliberate policy of foreign governments. Yet for almost ten years previously U.S. deficits were no problem. Clearly it is a change in human attitude and public policy, not inexorable circumstances, that has compelled us to take "corrective" actions.

It is true that the concern of financial officials about "the dollar" was only an echo—and a subdued echo at that—of the fears, hopes, anxieties, and speculations that arose in private financial circles in the late 1950s. But financial officials do not have to follow the private exchange markets; they can lead instead. By an equivocal attitude toward private suspicions of the dollar, European officials kept pressure on the United States.

Never did they firmly say that they would not force devaluation or suspension of gold payments. Instead, they succeeded in making the maintenance of gold–dollar convertibility at $35 per ounce a unilateral commitment of the United States, under three successive Administrations. Once a banker has solemnly assured the world and his depositors that he will never fail, he is at the mercy of those depositors capable of making him fail.

Memories are short, and gratitude is not a consideration respected in international relations, especially when money is involved. But the United States had and has considerable moral claim on European governments and central banks.

The present excess supply of dollars is in many respects an unwinding of the dollar shortage of the immediate postwar period. Capital left Europe because the continent was vulnerable to military attack, its governments were unstable, its industries were prostrate and uncompetitive, and its currencies were inconvertible. Capital has returned to Europe when events have overcome the special advantages which North America seemed to have in these respects. This is, probably, the main interpretation of the fact that one of the biggest negative items in our balance-of-payments accounts is the item called "unreported transactions" or "errors and omissions." For years this was a large positive item and was thought to reflect the transfer of European funds here by various devices. In the past few years it has been a large negative item, amounting to $1.5 billion in 1963. It is therefore relevant to recall the behavior of the United States when the shoe was on the other foot.

During the dollar shortage the United States: gave Western European countries (other than Greece, Turkey, and Spain) $32 billion of military and economic aid; lent them $11 billion additional (in spite of the default of European governments of debts connected with World War I); acquiesced in substantial devaluations of European currencies, without which European exports would still not be competitive; acquiesced in exchange controls, capital controls, quantitative restrictions on imports, and discriminations against the U.S. and other non-European countries —by no means all of which are liquidated even now. After enabling Europe to overcome the dollar shortage, the U.S. has been expected to adjust to its reversal *without* the tools that Europe used in its turn. Rightly so, because many of these tools were illiberal expedients—the more reason for replacing them now with compensatory intergovernmental finance.

The United States has undertaken, at considerable cost in real resources and foreign exchange, to defend Western Europe against the Soviet Union. This is in theory a joint effort, but European governments do not even yet fulfill their modest commitments to NATO. While European political leaders solicit constant reassurance that U.S. military power will remain visibly in Europe, their finance ministers and central bankers complain about the inflow of dollars.

The U.S. has not only tolerated but encouraged the development of a European customs union that attracts American capital and discriminates against American exports (especially the products of industries, notably agriculture, where North America has a clear comparative advantage).

The U.S. has borne a disproportionate share of the burden of assistance to uncommitted and underdeveloped nations, in which European countries have a common political and, one might hope, humanitarian interest.

The United States has provided a reserve currency. In the late 'forties no other international and intergovernmental money was available except gold, and the supply of gold was not keeping up with the demand. U.S. deficits filled the gap with dollars. It is true that this gave the U.S. a favored position among countries. Anyone who can print money can choose how new money will be first spent. The U.S. did not seek this privileged role; it arose by accidental evolution rather than conscious design. As it happens, the U.S. did not exploit it to live beyond our means, to make the American people more affluent. We used it rather for broad international purposes. No doubt in the long run the creation of new international money should be a privilege and responsibility more widely and symmetrically shared. But once the U.S. and the world are adjusted to the creation of international money via U.S. deficits, it is scarcely reasonable suddenly to ring a bell announcing that the world's financial experts have now decided that these deficits—past, present, and future—are pernicious.

The U.S. has not pushed its moral case before world public opinion. This is because many Americans believe, or prefer to believe, that balance-of-payments deficits, like venereal diseases, betray and punish the sins of those whom they afflict. Others regard them as simply matters of arithmetic and circumstance. Still others are afraid that making a moral argument will indicate to our all-powerful European creditors insufficient resolution to overcome the difficulties. On their side, the Europeans have neatly segregated the contexts. Their financial officials wash their hands of tariff and trade policies, agricultural protection, defense and aid appropriations, and their governments' budgets. Any European failings on these counts are facts of life to which the U.S. must adjust, rather than reasons for more patience or more credit.

By the narrowest of bankers' criteria—all moral claims aside —the United States is a good credit risk. Its balance sheet vis-à-vis the rest of the world, not to mention its internal productive strength, indicates capacity to service a considerably increased external public debt. The U.S. has been confined to the types of credit that can be given on the books of central banks. European parliaments cannot be asked to vote long-term loans to Uncle Sam, although the American people voted through the Congress to tax themselves to finance the Marshall Plan when Europe's credit rating was nil.

Meanwhile, European central banks are uneasy holding short-term dollar assets. They prefer gold. Why? Because they might some day force us to give them a capital gain on gold holdings. We compensate them with interest on their dollar holdings when they forego this speculative possibility. But bygones are bygones; and past interest earnings are irrelevant when future capital gains beckon. On its side, the U.S. has had nothing to lose and much to gain in guaranteeing to maintain the value of official dollar holdings. After stubbornly resisting this suggestion on obscure grounds of principle, the U.S. Treasury now belatedly and selectively guarantees value in foreign currency.

The only remaining reason to refuse the U.S. credit is that the United States, like any other deficit country, must be "disciplined."

Disciplined to do what?

To stop an orgy of inflation? The U.S. has the best price record of any country, except Canada, since 1958—before there was a balance-of-payments problem. The rates of unemployment and excess capacity during the period scarcely suggest that the government has been recklessly overheating the economy with fiscal and monetary fuel.

Nevertheless many Europeans say that when they buy dollars they are importing inflation. It is hard to take this claim seriously. First of all, if acquisitions of dollars are inflationary so are acquisitions of gold, and Europe shows no signs of saturation with gold. Second, the classic mechanism of international transmission of inflation is certainly not operating. We have not inflated ourselves into an import surplus adding to aggregate demand in Europe. To the contrary, we have maintained a large and secularly growing export surplus. Third, although central bank purchases of foreign exchange have the same expansionary monetary effects at home as other open-market purchases, it is not beyond the wit or experience of man to neutralize these effects by open-market sales or other monetary actions. Fourth, U.S. farmers and coal producers, and Japanese light manufacturers, among others, stand ready to help European governments reduce their living costs and their payment surpluses at the same time. The truth is that Europe does not really want a solution at the expense of its balance of trade.

Perhaps we are to be disciplined to cut foreign aid. European governments do not attach the same importance as we do to aid programs, especially in the Western Hemisphere. Clearly we need a better understanding on development assistance and "burden-sharing" among the advanced countries.

Should the United States be disciplined to cut off private exports of capital, by controls or by tight monetary policy or both? This has been a major and successful focus of European pressure. The U.S. authorities have responded by pushing up interest rates, more than a full point at the short end, and by proposing the Interest Equalization Tax. European pressure is motivated in part by nationalistic and protectionist aims—keep the rich Americans from buying up or competing with local industry. This may or may not be a worthy objective, but its worth is the same whether international payments are in balance or not.

Two other issues are involved. The first concerns capital markets and controls. Should the United States move toward poorer and more autarchic capital markets, or should the Europeans move toward more efficient and freer capital markets? Much of U.S. long-term capital movement to Europe does not represent a transfer of real saving. Instead it is a link in a double transatlantic chain connecting the European saver and the European investor. The saver wants a liquid, safe, short-term asset. The investor needs long-term finance or equity capital and seeks it in the United States. Unfortunately another link in the same chain is official European holding of short-term dollar obligations. But the Europeans themselves could, through institutional reforms, do a great deal to connect their savers and investors more directly and to reduce the spread between their long and short interest rates.

The second issue is the appropriate international level of interest rates. Evidently national rates must be more closely aligned to each other as international money and capital markets improve. But surely the low-rate country should not always do the aligning. This would impart a deflationary bias to the system. In principle easy fiscal policy could overcome this bias, but only at the expense of investment and growth. In the present situation European countries are fighting inflation by tightening their money markets rather than their budgets. They are forcing the U.S. to fight unemployment with a tight money–easy budget mixture. If interest rates are raised whenever a country faces either inflation or balance-of-payments difficulties, while expansionary fiscal policy is the only measure ever used to combat deflation, a number of swings in business activity and in payments will move the world to a mixture of policies quite unfavorable to long-run growth.

In summary, the adjustments forced on the United States to correct its payments deficit have not served the world economy well. Neither were they essential. European countries have had at their disposal several measures which are desirable in their own right, not just as correctives to the present temporary imbalance in payments. To the extent that they are unprepared to take these measures, they should willingly extend compensatory finance. International financial policy is too important to leave to financiers. There are more important accounts to balance than the records of international transactions, and more important markets to equilibrate than those in foreign exchange.

Chapter 15

Economic Progress and the International Monetary System

A great teacher of mine, Professor Joseph Schumpeter, used to find puzzling irony in the fact that liberal devotees of the free market were unwilling to let the market determine the prices of foreign currencies, and that opponents of government support of the price of wheat were strongly committed to government support of the price of gold. Thanks to the Bretton Woods Agreement of 1944, the Western world is committed to a system of fixed—or nearly fixed—rates of exchange among currencies and between currencies and gold. Market exchange rates are kept within 1 per cent of official parities by governmental purchases and sales in the exchange markets. Since the major currencies of North America and Western Europe can now (for all practical purposes) be freely bought and sold, one for another, considerable official intervention may at times be necessary to prevent a currency in high demand from appreciating more than the allowed 1 per cent, or to prevent a currency under selling pressure from depreciating beyond the permitted margin.

This is where international reserves come in. The international reserves of a country are essentially the resources it can quickly mobilize to buy its own currency and prevent it from depreciating. Clearly the need for international reserves is very largely a property of the system of fixed exchange rates. If countries were willing to entrust exchange rates entirely to private markets and to accept whatever gyrations in exchange rates might occur, they

Originally published in *Papers and Proceedings, Annual Meeting of the Academy of Political Science* (New York, May 1963), pp. 77–97.

would have no use for international reserves. There would be, by definition, no imbalances in international payments and no need for international money to move from the country in "deficit" to the country in "surplus." Instead the exchange rate would move—in favor of the country which would otherwise be in surplus—enough to bring market supplies and demands for the currencies into balance.

I do not propose to discuss here the merits of a system of market-determined flexible exchange rates as compared to the Bretton Woods system of fixed rates to which we are now committed. I propose rather to discuss the workability of the system we have.

Its workability depends essentially on two things: (1) the availability of international reserves permitting deficit countries to defend their exchange rates, and (2) the efficacy and speed of those corrective mechanisms that arrest and reverse flows of reserves from country to country. If the corrective mechanisms are strong and fast, the system can operate with small total reserves. If they are weak and slow, the system requires large reserves.

I shall discuss below the principal mechanisms that might be used to correct imbalances in international payments today, and I shall consider the limitations on their effectiveness or acceptability. But before getting to the specific list, I would like to offer four general observations on the process of international financial adjustment.

First, corrective mechanisms may be classified, in principle at least, into two groups: automatic and discretionary. Automatic mechanisms are economic processes that come into play as a result of imbalances in currency markets or as a by-product of the factors creating the imbalances. Discretionary mechanisms are policy actions taken by the governments concerned, designed to arrest or reverse outflows or inflows of reserves. The distinction is worth making, even though most of the automatic mechanisms are also discretionary, in the sense that government policy can moderate or suspend their operation.

Second, the mechanisms, automatic or discretionary, set into operation by payments deficits and surpluses are not necessarily or always corrective. They may aggravate, rather than correct, the initial disequilibrium. Economists are fond of self-correcting mechanisms. But we are far from having proved that a stable equilibrium in international payments exists, or that if it does exist it is speedily reached. We know, in fact, that some of the natural reactions of economies and of government policy-makers to disequilibrium may be destabilizing rather than stabilizing. I give a possible example below in discussing domestic deflation as a reaction to balance-of-payments deficits.

Third, pressures to take discretionary actions to correct imbalances are more keenly felt by deficit than by surplus countries. A country in deficit is forced to take action no later than when it exhausts its reserves and lines of credit. A country in surplus is under no similar compulsion. Indeed as a lender, a surplus country is in the driver's seat, able to exact adjustments by the deficit country as a condition of extending credit. Yet the appropriate corrections may involve adjustments at least as great in the economy and policy of the surplus country. One piece of financial ideology that obscures a dispassionate assessment of responsibilities for adjustment is the common facile assumption that balance-of-payments surpluses reflect financial virtue while deficits are the natural penalty for profligacy and sin. Often, no doubt, this judgment is justified. But sometimes the reverse is true. And most often, perhaps, serious imbalances of payments are the result of basic economic and political events and trends and reflect neither credit nor blame on either creditor or debtor.

The chief sanction inducing action by a surplus country is its awareness that balance-of-payments success is a transient glory, that some day it will sit in the debtor's chair. This reflection leads countries to grope collectively for some "rules of the game," which prescribe the behavior expected of good creditors as well as good debtors. The "rules of the game" are unwritten, informal, and uncertain. They are still in the process of development for the present monetary system of the West—evolving from gradual accumulation of precedents as well as from explicit consultation between governments and in the Organization for Economic Cooperation and Development, the Bank of International Settlements, and the International Monetary Fund.

The fourth point is the most fundamental. International monetary arrangements are not ends in themselves. They are means to more basic ends. Their ultimate purpose is to promote the economic progress of the free world, facilitating international commerce and the efficient use of the world's productive resources. In particular, the rationale of the Bretton Woods system is that stability of exchange rates eliminates a risk that would otherwise impede economically justified flows of goods and services and capital across national boundaries. It is essential not to lose sight of the basic objective and rationale of the system in appraising its various mechanisms of adjustment. The "rules of the game" should not force or even permit countries to defend their exchange rates by means which are inconsistent with the whole purpose of the system, i.e. by measures that retard world economic growth or restrict efficient movements of goods and services and capital.

In examining below the principal mechanisms of adjustment to imbalances in international payments, I shall ask in each case how effectively and speedily the mechanism can in today's world be expected to correct imbalances, and also how consistent the mechanism is with the essential objective and rationale of the system. I will anticipate here the conclusion I draw from this survey. The system does contain some effective and acceptable corrective mechanisms, but these certainly cannot be relied upon to operate quickly and powerfully. Major imbalances are likely to take years to eliminate, unless they are corrected by measures which hamper economic growth or restrict world commerce. Consequently, in my opinion, successful operation of the Bretton Woods system requires an adequate and growing stock of international liquidity, permitting countries to ride out prolonged periods of deficit.

In stating this conclusion, I run squarely into the debate between those who say the trouble with the international monetary system at present is lack of liquidity and those who say, on the contrary, that the trouble is simply the existing imbalances in payments. Certainly we have troubles on both counts. I want nothing I say to be interpreted to mean that any country, even the United

States, is able or should be able to run balance-of-payments deficits forever. No country can do so unless it possesses the printing press for creating international money, whether this takes the form of inexhaustible gold mines or some more rational and less costly equivalent. And no one country should possess such a printing press; this is a function that ought to be internationalized, for the same reasons that have led governments to nationalize the power of creating domestic money.

However, I do not find convincing the observation, so frequently repeated, that international liquidity would be ample if the system were only in balance-of-payments equilibrium. True enough, if we were always in equilibrium no reserves would be needed. But this is asking a great deal of the adjustment mechanisms. Every major imbalance may seem to be the last one—if we can only remedy this one, the system will have smooth sailing from now on. But the dollar shortage is succeeded by the dollar problem; Korea is followed by Suez, and Suez by Berlin and Cuba; the seemingly endless exchange troubles of France give way to an apparently chronic French surplus. The causes of imbalances are many—technological, economic, military, political. The only thing we can be sure of is that these causes will not all disappear, and that they will frequently represent and require deep-seated structural changes. If we are to weather the readjustments they impose within a system of fixed exchange rates, we will need both a large supply of international money in the future and improved international procedures for regulating this supply.

The details of such procedures are beyond the scope of this discussion. Let me say only that the technical details are secondary in importance and in difficulty to an understanding of the problem and a concerted will to resolve it. No more important aspect of international economic cooperation confronts the governments of the major advanced countries. If they do not solve it successfully and soon, then the Bretton Woods system will be a barrier rather than an avenue to economic progress and will eventually give way.

What are the mechanisms that correct imbalances in payments between countries in a regime of fixed exchange rates? What limitations on their use are imposed by other national and international objectives? How well and how fast can we expect the appropriate mechanisms to operate in the modern world?

1. *Changes in the employment of labor and industrial capacity.* I refer here to short-run changes in real income and employment, and correspondingly in the utilization of industrial capacity. These changes result mainly from variations in aggregate demand. An increased trade deficit—say, from a fall in export sales—automatically lowers aggregate demand both directly and indirectly through its "multiplier" effects on domestic incomes and expenditures. A reduction in aggregate demand lowers imports and frees domestic capacity to compete for foreign orders. Thus a rise in the trade deficit is partially self-correcting. But it is only partially so. If the trade balance is to be restored by reduction of aggregate demand, government fiscal and monetary policy must be actively restrictive.

All advanced countries are committed, almost without regard to political party, to full employment. Our friends in Western Europe are even more committed than we of North America. Deliberate deflation of aggregate demand, creating unemployment and excess capacity, is not a method of adjustment consistent with these commitments. Indeed, we must count it as a serious defect of our present system that countries where resources are idle for lack of effective demand, where no inflationary price increases are occurring, should feel themselves under pressure to adopt deflationary measures or to refrain from expansionary measures. For after all, the purpose of our economies is production; the purpose of international monetary arrangements is to promote the efficient use of productive resources; and the wastes of unemployment and unused capacity are the greatest of inefficiencies. Canada, faced by an exchange crisis last year, felt it necessary to take deflationary fiscal and monetary measures at a time when the internal economic situation indicated the contrary. The United States has for several years felt itself compelled to follow monetary policies inappropriate to the need for domestic expansion.

The usefulness of this mechanism is, therefore, doubtful because of the priority of the objective of full employment and full production. But in any case it is far from clear that the mechanism always corrects, rather than aggravates, the imbalance that sets it in motion. No doubt it tends to correct the balance of trade. But in the process it may push the balance of capital movements in the opposite and perverse direction. This is because profit performance and prospects, so important in the geographical placement of direct corporate investment and purchases of equities, are very sensitive to the level of business activity and utilization of capacity. I personally suspect that the failure of the U.S. economy to achieve full employment and full use of capacity during the late '50s and early '60s has lost us more in direct and equity investment capital outflow than it has gained us in the balance of trade.

2. *Changes in price levels.* Price increases in surplus countries, and price declines in deficit countries, are of course the classic mechanism of adjustment of the trade balance. These price-level adjustments are closely related to the movement of real economic activity just discussed; and they are set in motion by the same reactions of the economy and of government fiscal and monetary policy to external imbalance. However, this mechanism too has serious limitations.

First, price deflation is simply not a realistic possibility in modern industrial economies, and has not been for several decades. For a number of reasons, wages and prices are not flexible downward. Deflationary stimuli, whether from the trade balance itself or from government policy, will be reflected in reduction of employment and output far more than in reduction of prices. For the reason suggested above, contraction of real economic activity may not be favorable to the balance of payments as a whole.

Second, our countries seek stability of their internal price levels as well as full employment. Surplus countries are certainly not willing to undergo rapid and drastic inflation in order to draw in imports and damage the competitive position of their export industries.

This does not mean, fortunately, that price levels can be or need to be absolutely frozen in every country. We know that European money wages and prices have been rising in recent years somewhat faster than employment costs and prices in North America. This divergence in price trends will in time contribute to the correction of European surpluses and American deficits. But the process does take time, because European governments will not tolerate more than a modest upward creep in their price levels.

3. *Changes in monetary policy and interest rates.* Most national monetary systems, including our own, are geared to international reserves in such a way that domestic money is created to purchase inflowing gold and foreign currency, and destroyed when gold and foreign exchange are sold. If the authorities do not offset these transactions by other monetary measures, monetary conditions become easier and interest rates tend to fall in a surplus country, while the reverse is happening in a deficit country. The response of internationally mobile private funds to these changes in credit conditions and interest rates is a corrective mechanism, and sometimes a very powerful one. It is reinforced by the further effects of these monetary changes on domestic aggregate demand.

But this mechanism has its limitations.

First, the reallocation of private funds between national currencies is largely a one-time operation. The flow induced by a given interest rate differential will taper off. A country cannot expect to cover a basic deficit on current or long-term investment account indefinitely by attracting short-term money, unless it is prepared to jack its interest rates higher and higher.

Second, and more important, every country has domestic as well as external objectives for monetary policy. In many circumstances these will coincide, as when a country confronts simultaneously inflation at home and a deficit abroad. In other circumstances, like those of the United States today, the objectives diverge. Restrictive monetary policy would hold private funds here, but it would be generally deflationary. Correspondingly, a European surplus country could diminish its surplus by lower interest rates, but only at some risk of domestic inflation.

There are two ways in which the conflict between these objectives might be diminished. One is to dedicate monetary instruments to external balance, relying on fiscal measures for internal stabilization. Many Europeans have been urging the United States to tighten monetary policy, and to pursue a fiscal policy sufficiently expansionary to restore full employment even in the face of higher interest rates and tighter credit conditions. Correspondingly, European governments can be urged to combat whatever domestic inflationary problems they face by tightening budgets, while pursuing easier monetary policies in the interests of international balance.

The trouble is that every country imposes constraints, both economic and political, on the mixtures of monetary and fiscal medicine that can be administered. The proposed U.S. tax reduction looks to be about the largest dose of fiscal stimulant that is politically palatable in the United States. Moreover, domestic economic objectives going beyond full employment and countercyclical stabilization can limit the acceptable mixtures. For example, if we in this country place a high priority on private investment to promote long-run economic growth, we will not wish to suppress investment demand by tight money and high interest rates even if we could wholly compensate such restriction of demand by fiscal measures favoring consumption. Indeed we cannot even be sure that an easy-budget–tight-money mixture will benefit the balance of payments in the long run. For improvement in our trade balance depends on an accelerated advance in productivity, difficult to achieve in a low-investment economy.

The other way of reconciling the conflicting uses of monetary policy is to devise and to employ techniques of monetary control that serve both masters at once. United States monetary authorities and debt managers have for the past two or three years sought to keep short-term interest rates relatively high while increasing bank reserves and credit availability, and so far as possible lowering long-term interest rates. The assumption of this policy is that short rates are relatively more important for international flows of funds, and bank reserves, credit availability, and long-term rates relatively more important for domestic expansion. The techniques used have been (1) to increase the supply to the public of Treasury bills and other federal obligations of maturity less than one year, relative to other maturities of public debt—

the Federal Reserve has accordingly concentrated its open-market purchases in securities of maturity longer than one year; (2) to reduce bank reserve requirements in order to supply banks with new free reserves without open-market purchases; (3) to raise interest rates payable on commercial bank time and saving deposits, steering the bulk of the increase in bank deposits into this form rather than into demand accounts and giving the commercial banks an incentive to increase their holdings of mortgages, state and local bonds, and other long-term assets.

These policies have been moderately successful. In two years of recovery, short-term rates have risen by about ¾ of a point. Rates on longer-term federal obligations are virtually unchanged, and other long-term rates have fallen slightly. Conceivably this kind of policy could be pursued even more consistently and vigorously. For example, the Treasury appears to have acted counter to this policy in its successful efforts to place more of the federal debt in maturities beyond ten years.

But under the best of circumstances, these techniques can reduce somewhat but not wholly resolve the dilemma of the monetary and debt management authorities. Short- and long-term interest rates are linked by a chain of substitution that limits the degree to which the differentials between them can be altered. Furthermore, short rates are of some importance to domestic expansion and long rates of considerable relevance to international capital flows. The policy we have been following is a good compromise, but it is at best a compromise.

We cannot escape the fact that in a regime of convertible currencies the money and capital markets of different countries are closely linked. This means that countries have less scope for independent monetary policies than in the past. But we cannot escape either the fact that national monetary policies must be adapted to domestic circumstances, needs, and objectives which differ widely from country to country. In my view the major monetary powers will have to concert their monetary policies, through international consultation and cooperation, more than they have done in the past. If interest rates need to be brought into closer alignment, at what level should the alignment occur? Do the countries with high interest rates need to come down, or the countries with low rates go up? This is the kind of problem that has to be laid on the table when government officials and central bankers meet at Paris or Basel or Washington. At the same time, I am convinced that our international monetary arrangements must leave room for divergences in national monetary policies and interest rates to accommodate differences in domestic requirements. In many cases it will be easier for the central banks and governments concerned to offset private capital flows by official movements in the other direction than to adjust national monetary policies so as to shut off these flows altogether.

4. *Restrictions on private transactions in foreign exchange.* An instinctive reaction of a government to a balance-of-payments deficit is to restrict private transactions leading to purchases of foreign currency. The devices are too numerous to catalogue— the spectrum ranges from higher tariffs to a complete battery of exchange controls and includes import quotas, controls of capital movements, and restrictions on foreign travel. Needless to say, these expedients undermine the central purpose of a system of fixed exchange rates: to facilitate the international exchange of goods and services and the efficient use of productive resources throughout the world. Moreover, the prospect that countries will resort to these devices in times of balance-of-payments stress imposes risks on foreign commerce and foreign investment comparable to the risks of exchange depreciation. Once again we have, therefore, a clear danger of inverting ends and means. Exchange parities may be defended, but by means that subvert the whole purpose of defending them.

From this standpoint, recent actions of countries facing exchange crises are not encouraging. Canada imposed in 1962 special import surcharges, removing them the following year. The United Kingdom in 1961 tightened its controls over long-term capital exports. We ourselves cut down the duty-free import allowance for returning tourists.

Removal or liberalization of restrictions by surplus countries serves both to remedy imbalances in payments and to promote the basic objectives of the system. Indeed so long as this course is open to surplus countries, one is not disposed to sympathize with their complaint that the deficit countries are forcing inflation upon them. It is, of course, a great achievement that the tight network of quantitative controls and bilateral trade and clearing agreements which governed European commerce in the days of dollar shortage has now been largely dismantled. But some discrimination against U.S. goods remains, and the Common Market confronts us with new discriminations, especially in the important field of agriculture. European capital markets are, by and large, either controlled or poorly developed or both. Most governments other than the United States still regard control of private capital movements as a legitimate tool of balance-of-payments policy.

5. *Government transactions.* Largely because of foreign aid, foreign lending, and defense, government outlays and receipts now play a large role in international payments. They are obvious candidates for adjustment whenever a government faces a problem of imbalance. The principal reaction of the United States to its persistent deficit has been to economize on the government account: tying foreign aid to purchases in the U.S., increasing the preference given to American suppliers in defense procurement, cutting back the outlays for and by U.S. troops stationed abroad, negotiating for greater participation by our NATO allies in expenditures for the common defense. To a much lesser degree— reflecting the characteristic asymmetry between surplus and deficit countries—European surpluses have led European governments to increase their defense expenditures and their assistance to underdeveloped countries.

In practice the balance of payments has doubtless been the occasion for some economies and readjustments of burdens that were overdue on other grounds. But in principle these methods of adjustment are as objectionable on grounds of economic efficiency as the imposition of discriminatory controls or taxes on private outlays in foreign currency. A dollar of government outlay in foreign currency should not have to pass a more, or less, severe test than a dollar spent domestically. Nor should a dollar of government outlay in foreign currency have to pass a test more severe than a dollar of private outlay in foreign currency. One of the paradoxes of our present balance-of-payments difficulties is that stringent economies and controls are placed on government outlays abroad serving national purposes of the highest priority, while private individuals and firms can buy foreign currencies freely for any purpose—recreational travel, competitive investment abroad, or even speculating against the dollar. Nationalistic restrictions on government outlays may be justified as a temporary expedient. But such measures as aid-tying and "buy American" preferences will build up vested interests and be difficult to reverse.

The relative "burdens" of defense and development assistance of the various advanced countries should be related to their basic capacities to bear these burdens—as reflected in national income and wealth. Participation in these programs should not vary with the vagaries of national currencies. The effectiveness of the programs will be greatest, for a given collective cost to the participating countries, if the goods and services needed to implement the programs are bought in the cheapest markets.

6. *Changes of economic structure.* Under favorable circumstances certain basic economic processes will work toward the restoration of international balance. Let me give several examples:

—Specific industries challenged by foreign competition at home and abroad respond with better design, lower prices, or increased sales effort. The response of the American automobile industry to European imports is a case in point.

—High profits attract capital overseas and contribute to payments deficits. But these profit rates decline as the most obvious technological and market opportunities are grasped and as labor shortages are encountered. At the same time, repatriated earnings on the initial surge of foreign investments eventually strengthen the balance of payments. The United States already appears to be enjoying some relief of this kind.

—As comparative advantage shifts, a country suffers from new foreign competition in a particular industry, call it industry A. But as the surplus country shifts resources to industry A in order to exploit this opportunity, it leaves itself vulnerable to competition in other products. The deficit country can restore its overall payments position by shifting to these products the resources displaced by competition from industry A.

These fundamental adjustments depend on changes in relative prices and wages rather than on dramatic inflations or deflations of national price levels. They require changes in the composition of output rather than in aggregate production and employment. But they cannot be achieved without mobility of labor and other resources within each country. They are certainly neither easy nor quick.

7. *Adjustment of exchange rates.* Finally, the IMF agreement does not contemplate that exchange rates are eternally fixed. Rather the Bretton Woods system is a system of "adjustable pegs." A country can unilaterally alter its originally declared rate as much as 10 per cent. Further adjustment is permitted in case of "fundamental disequilibrium," with approval of the IMF. In practice, advance consultation with the IMF is considered impossible because of the dangers of speculation, and the approval of the IMF is perfunctory ratification of a fait accompli. Although each exchange rate adjustment is a specific national policy decision, dominated by the circumstances and needs of the individual country at the time, the frequency of such adjustments is an important property of the system as a whole. For it determines with what confidence or suspicion the world looks on any existing structure of exchange rates.

Frequent alterations of exchange rates between convertible currencies rob the system of its principal advantage over a system of freely floating rates. The merit of fixed exchange rates in promoting international trade and investment is to remove from these transactions the risk of exchange loss. But this risk is not removed if exchange rates are only temporarily pegged. Needless to say, exchange-rate stability is especially important for a currency, like the dollar, which is used as an international unit of account, medium of exchange, and store of value both by private individuals and businesses and by governments.

The possibilities of devaluation under the "adjustable peg" system inevitably lead to speculation, first against one currency, then against another. Any currency can be suspect, as we in the United States have been reminded several times during the past few years. The private resources available for such speculation in a regime of convertible currencies stagger the imagination. There is always a danger that speculative rumors and whims will be self-fulfilling. To guard against such danger, the central banks, governments, and international institutions which manage the "adjustable peg" system must command large counter-speculative resources.

This is the dilemma of exchange-rate policy. If the pegs are adjusted from time to time, currency speculation will be a major factor aggravating or even originating imbalances in international payments. If the pegs are never changed, we deny ourselves the use of an important instrument of adjustment, in many ways the simplest, most powerful, and least costly instrument. This means that the burden of correcting imbalances has to be assumed by more far-reaching and time-consuming processes of adjustment. Whichever exchange-rate policy is followed, large international reserves are necessary. In the one case, they are necessary to withstand the waves of speculation endemic to a system in which rates do in fact change from time to time. In the other case, they are necessary to permit a country to ride through a period of deficit which it must correct by slower and more difficult processes than devaluation. Thus I return to the conclusion with which I introduced this survey of possible mechanisms of adjustment.

Chapter 16

The Problem of International Liquidity

Every society must agree on a common money. What things will be generally acceptable to the members of the society in settlement of their obligations to one another? Anthropology and history record a remarkable variety of answers to this question: immovable stones, cattle, pieces of metal, cigarettes, pieces of paper. The decisive common property of these and other moneys is evidently not their intrinsic value, because money generally commands more human labor than either its utility to man in consumption or its cost of production would merit. The crucial property is simply the social agreement itself. In any society, A accepts money in payment for goods and services because, and only because, he knows that B will in turn accept money from him in return for things A needs and wants. The reason B accepts money is the same. Thus general acceptability, the essential property of money, is a circular phenomenon: something used as money is generally acceptable because it is generally acceptable. Given the social function which money serves, it is easy to understand why every society, primitive or advanced, reaches a consensus on things that can serve as means of payment. It is not so easy to understand or explain or predict what objects this social consensus will select. In this respect, money is like language—the important thing for a society is to agree on a common language; which language matters much less.

The society of nations, like any other society, needs a common money. Like individuals, the national governments of countries connected by trade and other economic transactions, must agree

Statement presented to the Joint Economic Committee, Congress of the United States, November 15, 1963.

on what things will be generally acceptable in settlement of their obligations to one another. In particular, in a regime of fixed exchange rates between national currencies, governments must agree on "international money," assets which they will always accept in payment for their own currencies. As in the case of tribes or nations, it matters less what they agree on than that they agree on something. For once again, the important thing is general acceptability. Country X will accept international money in settlement of its claims on country Y because, and only because, X is confident that this money can later be used to discharge debts it may incur to country Z. Given the essential circularity of the process, firm agreement by a handful of major countries is all that is needed to establish the general acceptability of a money in settling balances between national central banks.

The present international moneys are first, gold, and second, key national currencies (principally the dollar, but also, within limited groupings of nations, the pound sterling and the French franc). Gold accounts for roughly two thirds, and national currencies one third, of national monetary reserves. National central banks have accepted gold and U.S. dollars in payment of their claims on other nations, because they think they will be able to use gold to discharge their own obligations in the future. Gold owes this status largely to historical tradition. But the standing promise of the United States to buy gold for dollars is an assurance to other countries that gold will command goods and services available in the United States. Dollars came to be accepted as international money partly because of the heavy demands of the rest of the world for U.S. products, properties, and securities in the 1940s and early 1950s and partly because of the U.S. commitment to foreign central banks to convert their dollars into gold on demand.

There are difficulties in operating a monetary system with two or more moneys convertible into each other on demand—difficulties exemplified on the one hand by the "dollar shortage" of World War II and the few years following, when the rest of the world preferred dollars to gold and dumped gold into the United States Treasury, and, on the other hand, by the reversal of this preference during recent years.

Two important questions to ask about any kind of money, national or international, are these: (1) How is the supply increased? (2) Who is the initial beneficiary of the increase in supply?

In the case of gold, the growth of the monetary supply depends mainly on new production in the West and on sales by the Soviet Union. New production outside the Communist bloc evidently cannot increase the monetary gold stock more than $2\frac{1}{2}$ per cent per year, even if it all goes into monetary use. Continuation of this rate of production is subject to the hazards of political instability in the Union of South Africa, the major producing country. Soviet gold sales have been running at about $250 million per year, less than 1 per cent of the monetary gold stock of the West. Once again prediction is hazardous. In recent years nearly half of new gold has gone into private uses and hoards. Private dishoarding could significantly increase the flow of gold into monetary reserves for a few years, provided that those who have been speculating in gold (at considerable sacrifice of income from alternative investment possibilities) become convinced that its price will never be raised.

The initial beneficiaries of an increase in the stock of monetary gold are the gold-mining countries, which are able to buy with newly mined gold the things they want (grain, for example) from the rest of the world. These countries can, in effect, run chronic deficits in their balances of payments, financing them with gold. It is somewhat ironical that the principal beneficiaries of our monetary use of gold are countries that we would scarcely be inclined to aid by grants or loans.

The same two questions may be asked about reserve currencies. How do dollars find their way into the monetary reserves of central banks? This happens when Americans, and foreigners who have acquired dollars in transactions with Americans, offer dollars for foreign currency, let us say French francs, in the exchange market. If not enough private purchasers come forward to buy these dollars, the Bank of France is obliged to step into the breach to keep the franc from appreciating against the dollar. If the Bank of France is content to hold the dollars, rather than to ask for gold, then world monetary reserves have increased;

the French hold more international money, and neither the United States nor any other country holds less. Thus it is an excess supply of dollars, stemming from current or past deficits in the U.S. balance of payments, which increases the stock of dollars in world monetary reserves.

Here, however, we have the dilemma to which my colleague Professor Robert Triffin called the world's attention in 1958. It is not possible to increase the supply of reserve currencies beyond some point without endangering the stability of the gold-exchange system. If the reserve-currency country continues in deficit, its demand liabilities rise relative to the gold available to meet them and its creditors become uneasy. But if it succeeds in stemming the flow of its currency to other central banks, then total reserves in this form will cease to grow. Throughout the 1950s dollar accumulations by foreign central banks were the major source of expansion in world monetary reserves. Some time around 1959 or 1960, however, dollar deficits ceased to expand the *effective* supply of world liquidity. This is not because the deficits ceased, but because the United States had to begin to worry about its liabilities to foreign central banks, in effect to reckon its own monetary gold reserves *net* of these liabilities. It was no longer true that accumulation of dollars abroad left U.S. reserves unchanged. Once this revolution in attitudes had occurred, the reserve-currency mechanism for increasing the effective supply of international money ceased to function.

Under the reserve-currency system properly functioning, the initial beneficiary of an increase in the supply of international money is obviously the reserve-currency country itself. It is pleasant to have a mint or printing press in one's backyard, and the gold exchange standard gave us, no less than South Africa, this privilege. We were able to run deficits in our balance of payments for ten years because our IOUs were generally acceptable as money. No one worried about those deficits. They did not appear to be a problem until the acceptability of the money we were "printing" to finance them came into question.

The United States need not apologize for the manner in which we used the privilege of coining international money. We did not use it to live beyond our means, or to promote purely American interests. We did not use it to go on a binge of inflation, contaminating the rest of the world. We used it for international purposes—for the common defense, development assistance, for long-term investments in capital-hungry economies all over the world.

Nevertheless, we must recognize that we have neared the end of this particular road. We no longer own a printing press for international money. Whatever technique the major countries may now develop for the creation of new international money will be more symmetrical as between nations. The privilege of putting new money into international circulation will be shared, rather than concentrated on one country. It is important that the international responsibilities which the United States has associated with this privilege be shared as well.

I have spoken so far of the prospects for expansion in the supplies of the two kinds of international money that dominate the present system. The prospective expansion of effective monetary gold and dollar reserves does not match the growth in trade and production that we expect and hope. While world trade and international transactions grow at perhaps 5 or 6 per cent per year, gold will probably be adding less than 2 per cent per year to the stock of reserves, and dollars will be adding effectively nothing at all.

I do not regard this comparison as conclusive proof of an impending shortage of liquidity, because the aggregate demand of central banks and governments for international monetary reserves is only loosely related to the growth of the world economy. I do not believe in a mechanical connection between economic activity and money on a national level, and certainly not on an international plane either. It is quite possible that ways will be found to economize international money. Nevertheless, I think there is a considerable risk that there will be, if there is not already, a shortage of international money under present international monetary arrangements.

Why does a country need international reserves? The principal reason is this: In a regime of fixed exchange rates, a country is obliged to buy its own currency in the foreign exchange markets to keep its exchange rate from falling. (Under the Bretton Woods system a country must keep the rate within 1 per cent of the officially declared parity.) The government or central bank must be prepared to buy its own currency with foreign currencies. The country's monetary reserves either provide it directly with foreign currency to sell—e.g. when the reserves are in dollars—or provide it with the means of obtaining the needed currency from other governments, as when the reserves are in gold. When a country is in balance-of-payments deficit, the demand for its currency is less than the supply at the fixed rate. The government or central bank has to make up the difference. Therefore, the quantity of reserves a country needs, or believes it needs, depends on the size and duration of the deficits in its balance of payments that it may have to finance.

If international payments were always perfectly balanced, there would be no need for international reserves. But if there are large swings of long duration in payments balances, then countries need large reserves in order to finance them. Therefore, to appraise the need for international reserves, it is necessary to consider the magnitude of the swings which countries should be prepared to finance. There are two parts to this question. The first concerns the causes of these swings. The second concerns the strength and speed of mechanisms, both in the economies of the countries affected and in their policies, which work to correct and reverse imbalances in international payments.

The sources of swings in international payments are numerous and various. Changes in technology and in taste can alter the competitive positions of different nations in trade and change the relative attractiveness of various areas for capital investment. Political and military events can alter the risks of holding wealth in one country relative to another. Business cycles can be out of phase as between countries. Labor forces and their productivities can grow at different rates. National policies can differ. The list could be extended in great detail.

It may be that the basic sources of imbalance—now in one direction, now in another—will be less important relative to the size of world trade and the world economy in the next decade than they have been in the past fifteen to twenty years. But it would not be prudent to base policy on so optimistic an assumption. This is especially true because we may not yet have experienced the full impact on the mobility of private capital of establishment in 1958 of convertibility between major currencies.

Assuming that imbalances continue to arise, how strong are the policies and mechanisms that can correct and reverse them? The more effective and speedy these policies and mechanisms, the less need there will be for international reserves with which to finance deficits. I cannot go into detail on this difficult question, which I have tried to deal with elsewhere:[1] To summarize, I believe that the *acceptable* policies and mechanisms cannot be expected to correct imbalances very quickly. I emphasize the word *acceptable,* because there are always some expedients that a country can employ to bring its accounts into balance, which indeed a deficit country is forced to employ as it exhausts its reserves and other means of financing. But these expedients are often unacceptable, in the sense that they undermine the national and international objectives that it is the very purpose of the international monetary system to promote. Indeed, the major symptom of a shortage of international liquidity would be—and perhaps already is—that countries resort to such expedients.

All the major monetary countries are committed to full employment and to economic growth. If each successive deficit country is forced to retard its economy and to waste its resources in unemployment and excess capacity in order to conserve its international reserves, then the international monetary system is not promoting but is obstructing a basic goal of policy. Similarly, the purpose of fixed exchange rates is to promote efficient trade and capital investment across national boundaries. If exchange controls, or special import quotas and duties, or preferences to domestic suppliers, are imposed for balance-of-payments reasons, then once again the servant has become the master—fixed exchange rates are preserved but the purpose of fixing them is sacrificed. If governments have to cut back on programs of great national importance simply because of their costs in foreign currency, they are being forced to adjust to balance of payments deficits too fast.

1. See Chapter 15.

Under the Bretton Woods system, a country may adjust to a "fundamental disequilibrium" by devaluing its currency. But frequent use of this expedient robs the system of the major advantage of fixed exchange rates—that they permit traders and investors to make transactions within and across national boundaries free of the risks of changes in exchange rates. Moreover, changes in exchange parities can be self-defeating, from the standpoint of the reserve needs of the system as a whole, because they incite speculative movements of funds between currencies.

There are acceptable mechanisms and policies of adjustment that do not conflict with more basic economic and political objectives. For example, a deficit country with over-full employment and inflation can remedy both its internal and its external difficulties by more restrictive monetary and fiscal policies. Unfortunately, although it dominates much thinking on the subject, this is by no means the only kind of imbalance that occurs. Other kinds of imbalance require difficult, far-reaching, and slow changes in economic structure, during which the deficit country needs enough reserves or credit to defend its exchange parity.

When there is a world shortage of liquidity, the burden of adjustment to imbalances falls disproportionately on the deficit countries. The surplus countries have a much smaller incentive to take actions to arrest or reverse the inflow of reserves. Instead, they are glad to build up their reserve positions against the day when events beyond their control will place them in a deficit position.

It is true that accumulation of monetary reserves is an unprofitable investment for a nation, and beyond some point the country will prefer to use these resources to import goods for domestic consumption or investment and to acquire less liquid but higher yielding foreign assets. But as nations advance in prosperity they can better afford the luxury and security of accumulating reserves. This phenomenon is another reason for expecting the demand for reserves to increase at least as fast as the world economy grows. It is not too difficult to divide the world between (1) countries that live on a hand-to-mouth basis, spending fairly promptly all the foreign exchange they can acquire, and (2) countries that accumulate and decumulate reserves as their balance-of-payments fortunes fluctuate. The first category includes the poorer and less developed countries. The second category has been gaining members since the war as national standards of living have improved.

The "right" amount of aggregate international liquidity would give surplus countries as great an incentive to take actions to stem the inflow of reserves as deficit countries have to stem the outflow. The burden of adjustment to payments imbalances would be symmetrically shared. It is in this sense—that the burden falls disproportionately on deficit countries and forces them to take undesirable measures—that there is today and may well be tomorrow a shortage of international liquidity.

An excess of liquidity is conceivable. The symptoms would be the opposite of those of a shortage. Surplus countries would feel a disproportionate pressure to adjust—e.g. by lowering interest rates, acquiescing in inflation, appreciating their currencies, or spending foreign currencies freely on government programs. Deficit countries would be too free of discipline. This is not an immediate danger. But it is a reason for making sure that the creation of international money is under control, whatever form it takes, so that the supply does not outrun the demand.

Evidently there is good reason to believe (1) that the effective supplies of principal kinds of international money—gold and official dollar balances—cannot keep pace with world trade and production, and (2) that demands for international liquidity will grow at least as fast as the world economy. Moreover, it is by no means clear that the supplies are even today adequate. How can this gap be filled?

I referred earlier to the possibility that the major monetary countries can find ways to use international money more efficiently. International *liquidity* is a broader concept than international *money*. It includes facilities for the granting of credit from one country, or group of countries, to another. To the extent that deficit countries can count on receiving such credit, they have less need for reserves.

During 1960–63 an impressive network of lines of credit between governments and central banks has been constructed, thanks in large part to the initiative and imagination of the United

States Treasury and the Federal Reserve System. These new arrangements have considerably strengthened the hands of the participating countries in dealing with temporary swings from one currency to another due to speculation or other quickly reversible causes.

But credit facilities are an imperfect substitute for reserves. They generally provide liquidity conditional on the consent of the lenders, while owned reserves provide unconditional liquidity. Lenders are, after all, "in the driver's seat." They may refuse to grant credit or to extend it, or they may require as a condition the adoption of certain policies by the borrowing country. Anticipating this, a country may well seek to acquire unconditional reserves just so that it will not have to ask for credit when its currency is under pressure.

Consequently the liquidity gap will, in my opinion, have to be filled at least in part by new species of international money. The liabilities of the International Monetary Fund constitute an obvious candidate for this role. Member countries now possess virtually unconditional rights to draw certain amounts from the Fund in convertible currencies. (They also have conditional lines of credit for additional amounts.) These automatic drawing rights should be regarded as international reserves. There are various devices by which they could (1) be made more easily transferable from one country to another, and (2) be systematically and gradually increased in total amount. These devices do not require radical or abrupt changes in the IMF or other existing institutions. They would lead eventually to an international money whose supply would be under international control, not subject to the vagaries of gold production and gold hoarding or to fluctuations in the payments positions of reserve-currency countries. The initial disposition of newly created IMF drawing rights could be shared in an agreed and equitable manner among the members, not concentrated in gold-mining or reserve-currency countries.

The problem is important. If the major monetary countries have the will to solve it, the technical means are not hard to find.

Chapter 17

The Future of the Dollar as International Money

As General de Gaulle has characteristically reminded us in a recent press conference, the United States dollar occupies a unique position among national currencies. It is used as money throughout the world, not just in the country of issue. Will the dollar continue to perform this special international role, lately called into question by events as well as by the General? Does the United States have a national interest in the perpetuation of this external use of its currency? In what alternative ways could the international functions of the dollar be performed?

Foreign users of dollars are both *private* (banks, businesses, and individuals) and *official* (central banks, governments, and international institutions). For reasons that I shall develop, I believe there are good prospects for continuation and even expansion of private uses of dollars. However, I think the dollar is likely to lose sooner or later its position as a "reserve currency" for central banks and governments. I shall explain why I feel we should not be dismayed by this development, and I shall discuss some suggestions for replacing the dollar in the international monetary system.

Today foreign holdings of dollars amount to $24 billion, of which private holdings represent $11 billion and official holdings $13 billion. I exclude international institutions, which hold another $5 billion. I refer to foreign holdings of *dollars,* but of course I do not mean dollars in the literal sense of coin and currency. Very little takes that form. Rather I am speaking of obligations to foreigners payable on demand or within a year by U.S. banks or the U.S. Treasury. Increases in these liquid short-term liabilities

Delivered as Carl Snyder Memorial Lecture at the University of California, Santa Barbara, March 1965.

to foreigners are what we count, together with outflows of gold, as deficits in our balance of payments.

Foreign Private Dollar Holdings

Why do private banks, businesses, and individuals abroad hold dollars rather than their own national currencies? Sometimes, of course, they are speculating that their own currency may depreciate in value. Normally, however, these dollar holdings are working balances, maintained in preparation for making future dollar payments. They are analogous to the working bank balances of American households or corporations. The dollar is the unit of account, and medium of exchange, not only for the $40 billion of annual payments by foreigners to U.S. residents but for many other transactions in which neither party is a U.S. resident.

The dollar plays this role for several reasons. One is simply the size of the country and of its transactions with the rest of the world. Another is historical. After the Second World War, the dollar and the Swiss franc were the only currencies convertible on demand into any other national currency. Other currencies were subject to all kinds of exchange controls and to considerable risks of devaluation. The dollar's value was assured, less by U.S. possession of almost all the world's monetary gold in the free world than by the seemingly inexhaustible appetite of foreign countries for U.S. products. In these circumstances it was natural for exporters and importers, lenders and borrowers, to make their contracts in dollars.

A third reason is the high state of organization and efficiency of U.S. financial institutions and financial markets. The holder of a working balance naturally seeks to earn some interest return on his funds. Likewise, he wishes to be able to put funds in or take them out at any time conveniently, inexpensively, and quickly. The only places that really offer such facilities, through banks and a short-term money market, are New York and London. The checkered career of sterling since 1931 has confined its use as international money pretty much to the "sterling area," composed mainly of Commonwealth and ex-Commonwealth countries.

The Euro-Dollar Market

During recent years, it is true, strong competition with New York has developed in London and elsewhere in Europe. The new institutions and markets pay the dollar the sincerest kind of flattery. For they deal in "Euro-dollars," i.e. short-term liabilities to pay dollars, undertaken by foreigners rather than by American residents. When the debtor is a reputable London bank, his promise to pay dollars is virtually as good as "real" dollars in New York.

Euro-dollars are substitutes for real dollars just as bank deposits are substitutes for the coin and currency that they are obligations to pay. Thus the development of Euro-dollars has reduced world demand for dollars—not, of course, one-for-one. Banks and other dealers who have undertaken Euro-dollar obligations presumably keep some genuine New York dollars as reserves. Otherwise they might have to scramble to raise the dollars needed to meet their dollar-denominated obligations when they come due.

Of course they make loans expressed in dollars too. But, as in any banking operation, the loans are less liquid and more risky, as well as higher yielding, than the deposits. This difference is responsible both for the profit in the operation and for the need for fractional reserves. I don't know what the reserve fraction is in the Euro-dollar market, but it is probably quite low. Even if it were as high as one fifth, every Euro-dollar substituted for a real dollar in international working balances would mean a net reduction of 80 cents in the demand for dollars.

The major attraction of Euro-dollars has been that they pay a higher interest rate than deposits in New York or U.S. Treasury bills. At the same time, Euro-dollar market banks are able to make loans at rates competitive with U.S. lenders. The profit opportunity which has called for the Euro-dollar market is the gap between deposit interest rates and loan interest rates in the United States. This gap was in part due to the legal ceiling imposed in the U.S. on the rates commercial banks may pay on time deposits. Although the Federal Reserve has raised this ceiling in several steps over the past three years, it still handicaps the U.S. in the international competition for funds. The ceiling should be abandoned altogether.

So far as foreign demand for dollars is concerned, the obvious reduction due to substitution of Euro-dollars is offset only to the extent that fractional dollar reserves are held against Euro-dollars, which are substituted for holdings of other national currencies. The offset cannot be large, although I do not know of any successful attempts to pierce the mysteries of the Euro-dollar market and measure these effects.

The economy of dollars accomplished by the Euro-dollar market is by its nature a once-for-all phenomenon. The dollar may already have survived the main blow it is going to suffer from this source. Once the initial profit opportunity is exploited—and Euro-dollar rate margins are very narrow now—the market will grow at roughly the same pace as the world economy, and so will its need for genuine dollar reserves.

Besides the competition of Euro-dollars, adverse speculation has reduced private demand for dollars in recent years. In spite of these two disadvantages, private dollar holdings abroad have been rising by about $1 billion a year. This seems to me impressive testimony of the strength of the world economy's normal demands for dollars for working balances. In satisfying these demands, we can probably run a balance-of-payments deficit, according to the Commerce Department definition of the term, of $1.5 billion a year without putting the dollar under pressure in the foreign exchange markets.

Official Dollar Holdings

I turn now to the official use of dollars. Some official holdings are working balances, similar to the private holdings I have just been discussing. The central banks of other countries are committed, under the Articles of Agreement of the International Monetary Fund, to maintain the values of their currencies in the foreign exchange markets within 1 per cent of the declared official parities. They do this by buying or selling dollars for their own currencies. They have working balances of dollars both as a result of and in anticipation of their interventions in the exchange markets.

But the current dollar holdings of foreign central banks and governments greatly exceed their needs for working balances. The dollar has been used as a "reserve currency," and the bulk of official holdings abroad represent reserves that nations hold against adverse development which threaten their exchange rates or their ability to pay for needed imports.

Gold is the most important reserve asset. But, especially after the Second World War, many nations began to use dollars in place of gold or in combination with gold. Dollars could earn interest; they were directly usable in the foreign exchange markets; they were convertible into gold at the U.S. Treasury; they commanded American goods and services. Until the late 'fifties, therefore, the U.S. could count on foreign central banks to hold gladly any dollars that came their way.

This buildup of dollar reserves, moreover, served an important international purpose. Without them, Europe and the rest of the world could have built up their own reserves only by depleting the U.S. gold stock. This would have forced the U.S. to take, early in the postwar period, deflationary and restrictive measures. New gold production is not able to keep pace with the demand for reserves in a growing world economy.

The reserve-currency system grew like Topsy; it was never deliberately and consciously created. But its internal logic is that foreign countries will accept unlimited quantities of dollars in payment for their goods and their properties. As General de Gaulle and his unofficial monetary adviser, M. Jacques Rueff, have so eloquently pointed out, the principle of the reserve-currency system is indefensible. It is as if an individual citizen of the United States had the power to print dollar bills for his own use. We have long since centralized and nationalized the power to create national currency. For similar reasons General de Gaulle is unassailable when he asks that international money "not bear the mark of any individual country."

Of course the reserve-currency system has not been operating according to its internal logic in recent years. On the contrary, the United States has been faced ever since 1960, at the latest, with the distinct possibility that General de Gaulle and others will ask us to convert into gold not only the dollars currently accruing to them but also those which they happily accepted in the halcyon days of the reserve-currency system. This has made our supposedly privileged position much less comfortable, to say the least, than it would be if dollars really continued to be the unquestioned equivalent of gold.

I do not think it is simply nationalistic bias that leads me to assert that the U.S. did not abuse the privileged position of owning a printing press for international money. We did not flood European countries with worthless paper, forcing them into inflation while we carted home the products of their toil and thrift. On the whole, we used our international monetary privilege to finance the responsibilities we had assumed in the common defense of the West and in assistance to the underdeveloped world.

It is true that American investors have been acquiring large and presumably profitable industrial and commercial interests in Europe. As a nation, we have financed these acquisitions by pouring dollars into European central banks. It would be hard to judge whether this is an abuse of the reserve-currency system, or whether it is a result of the formation of a customs union that at the same time attracts American capital and excludes American exports. But in any event a European country with nationalistic objections to the U.S. capital invasion can handle the problem by direct measures. Were the international monetary system otherwise satisfactory, the fact that it has facilitated this movement of capital would not be a reason for changing it. Indeed facilitation of capital movements is one of the principal *raisons d'être* of the system of fixed exchange rates.

But it is really beside the point to argue whether or not the U.S. has abused, or is abusing, its reserve-currency status. General de Gaulle's monetary restlessness is of a piece with his general restlessness, shared in some measure by other European governments. Europe will no longer accept without question and participation U.S. international leadership, no matter how benevolent. We will undoubtedly have to construct more symmetrical arrangements for making international decisions and sharing international responsibilities in the fields of defense and foreign aid, as well as more symmetrical international monetary arrangements.

Some countries, particularly those in the Western Hemisphere, may continue to find it in their interest to hold the bulk of their reserves in dollars because of their close trading ties with the United States. Similar arrangements exist within the sterling area, and within the franc zone, which includes most of France's former dependencies in Africa.

In particular, the United States and Canada may find it in their mutual interest to move toward a monetary union. We would give Canada a large line of credit; in return Canada would agree to hold all its reserves, above a minimal gold stock, in U.S. dollars. This would formalize what is already true, i.e. that a consolidated North American balance of payments is of much greater relevance to the strength of the two dollars than their separate accounts. Capital outflows across our northern border should not really be a cause for concern about the U.S. dollar, as they are in present statistical practice. Such outflows tend to be offset sooner or later by Canadian imports from the U.S. or by increased holdings of dollars by the Bank of Canada.

Outside a "dollar area," however, I believe that we in the United States must face squarely the inevitable prospect that other countries will cease to hold dollars as official reserves above minimal working balances. They will insist on a more symmetrical or neutral international money. Recent French conversions of dollars into gold are a dramatic indication. Perhaps the handwriting on the wall can be read even more clearly from the unobtrusive way in which Germany, which has no political reason to embarrass the U.S., has been steadily reducing the dollar content of its reserves. And even when conversions are not made, the threat hangs over our heads like the sword of Damocles and forces us to take all kinds of measures that conflict with U.S. foreign and domestic policy.

Alternatives to the Reserve-Currency System

What could take the place of the dollar in official reserves? And how could the transition to a new kind of international money be arranged?

The Gold Standard. One proposal, of course, is to adopt a pure gold standard. Nations would hold only gold metal as international reserves. Balance-of-payments deficits resulting in claims by one central bank upon another would be settled in gold. Presumably central banks and governments might extend each other credit. But deficit countries would have no automatic or presumptive rights to such credit. This is the system favored by Jacques Rueff, among others.

Any abrupt institution of the gold standard would involve massive conversion of dollars into gold. U.S. gross reserves would decline drastically, and total world reserves would contract by an equivalent amount. To avoid this shock, most advocates of the gold-standard solution favor an increase in the price of gold in terms of all currencies. By marking up the value of its gold stock by 66⅔ per cent, the U.S. would be able to pay off $10 billion of its short-term debts in gold and still have, as now, $15 billion in gold reserves. Other countries' reserves would be increased by two thirds of their current gold stocks. Most gold-standard advocates would regard this expansion of world reserves as inflationary. They would prefer an increase in gold price of the order of 33⅓ per cent, which would be just sufficient to enable reserve currency holdings outside the currency "areas" to be replaced by gold without changing the total of world reserves. In this case the U.S. would have only $10 billion in gold left after the two operations: revaluation of our stock to $20 billion and conversion of $10 billion of outstanding dollars. Our loss of $5 billion in reserves would be balanced by increases in the reserves of other countries.

All major governments have repeatedly opposed this solution and expressed their determination to avoid it. The main national beneficiaries would be South Africa and the Soviet Union, the principal gold producers. The main private beneficiaries would be the gold speculators and hoarders who have already caused so much trouble. A rise in the gold price now would encourage similar speculation and hoarding some time in the future. It would put more world resources into an essentially wasteful activity, and even so there would be little prospect that gold production would augment reserves at a sufficiently rapid or regular rate to meet the needs of an expanding world economy. Surely in this day and age man can contrive a better solution than to reinforce the ancient irrational myth of gold.

The Collective Reserve Unit. The French government has promoted discussion of one alternative scheme, the Collective Reserve Unit or CRU, and I suspect this, rather than a literal metallic gold standard, was in the back of General de Gaulle's mind. In its essence the proposal would increase the value of gold in official monetary gold stocks, but not the value of unmined or privately hoarded gold. CRUs, which may be regarded as paper gold, would be issued to participating nations roughly in proportion to their gold stocks. They would be issued by an agent—the French propose the Bank of International Settlements in Basel—with whom the participating countries would deposit equivalent amounts of their own currency. Thus a CRU would represent, say, 50 cents in U.S. dollars, 10 cents in French francs, 12 cents in German marks, and so on. Deficits would be settled in gold-cum-CRUs in fixed proportions corresponding to their shares in aggregate reserves.

CRUs would replace dollars in monetary reserves. Assuming that the initial issue was designed to change the form but not the total of reserves, it would be about one third of the aggregate monetary gold stock and have the same effect on U.S. and foreign reserve positions as a 33⅓ per cent increase in the price of gold.

The CRU proposal has two great merits. It would be a truly international fiduciary money, based on a portfolio of national currencies rather than any single national money. It is vastly superior to gold, because no resources need be wasted in producing it; and its supply can be deliberately controlled rather than left to the accidents of mining economics and technology and the whims of private hoarders and the Soviet Union. Nevertheless, the proposal has decisive disadvantages for the world, and particularly for the United States.

First, the French wish to confine the participating group of nations to a big boys' club—ten or twelve leading monetary powers. These countries would print more money for themselves, and from this new mine of paper gold the rest of the world would benefit only indirectly. There already exists a worldwide monetary organization, the International Monetary Fund. The French proposal would diminish its importance by entrusting the most important monetary function to a select group, outside or only nominally inside the Fund.

Second, replacement of existing dollar holdings with CRUs, of which the dollar component is only fractional, inflicts on the United States a considerable loss of total reserves. As I argued above, the U.S. need have no apologies for the past. Its deficits were incurred for good international purposes and were essential to the international monetary system. We should insist that any new system consolidate the past without penalizing the United States. The first installment of CRUs should be backed 100 per cent by the dollars they replace in foreign reserves.

Third, the proposal has a restrictive and deflationary spirit and bias. This is not intrinsic to the proposal but reflects the French view that the current total of world reserves will be adequate for some time to come. They wish the new system to function like the gold standard described above; countries would have very little access to credit to relieve the necessity of settling deficits with metallic or paper gold.

In principle, the participating countries could regulate the supply of world reserves by agreeing to issue themselves, from time to time, new CRUs in the agreed national proportions. But since this would require a unanimous vote, doubts would probably be resolved by doing nothing.

The International Monetary Fund. The major alternative is to replace dollars with credits against the International Monetary Fund. The Fund already is a pool of national currencies from which members can draw. Some of their drawing rights are automatic; these should be, and increasingly are, regarded by member countries as international reserves on virtually the same plane as gold and reserve currencies.

These automatic rights arise in two ways. First, 25 per cent of members' quotas are subscribed in gold, the remainder in their own currencies. The gold "tranche" is automatically available. The total of gold tranche rights is now about $3.5 billion, and it will rise to about $4.5 billion under the 25 per cent increase in Fund quotas that has just been negotiated. Gold tranche drawing rights do not augment world reserves, since they only replace the gold paid into the Fund by member governments.

Second, a fiduciary creation of automatic drawing rights occurs as a by-product of Fund lending operations. For example, in the past when the Fund lent dollars to other members, typically underdeveloped countries, the United States obtained new automatic drawing rights—so-called pre- or super-gold-tranche rights —in equal amount. To the extent that the borrowing countries were using not solely the gold tranche of their quotas but the non-automatic credit tranches, the new automatic rights created for the U.S. were not offset by any reduction in the automatic rights of other members. In recent years the U.S. was able to use more than $1 billion of rights previously accumulated in this way to finance its balance-of-payments deficits. At present, the net automatic rights of Fund members thus created amount to about half a billion dollars.

There are several ways in which the IMF could create more reserves than it has in the past. One is to make another 25 per cent of quotas, the first "credit tranche," as automatic as the gold tranche. This would increase world reserves by more than $4 billion initially. It would also mean that future increases in quotas would add to world reserves *more* than they subtract in gold subscriptions.

A second device, which also has considerable appeal to me, is for the Fund to engage in investment operations. The Fund would purchase national currencies with pre-gold-tranche drawing rights. Members would share in these purchases in fixed proportions, probably governed by their relative quotas in the Fund. Fixing the proportions has the advantage of avoiding highly arbitrary political decisions each time an operation is undertaken. It makes these reserve-creating investments essentially neutral monetary operations, like the open-market operations of national central banks. They would be clearly distinct from extensions of credit to help individual countries, which are analogous to the discounting functions of national central banks.

There may be objections to Fund investments in the obligations of members with inconvertible currencies, which are not usable in Fund drawings. To meet these objections while still giving the underdeveloped world a share in the benefits of Fund reserve creation, an appropriate proportion of Fund investments could be reserved for purchase of the obligations of the International Bank or its affiliates.

Finally, it is essential to avoid total inaction whenever there is disagreement. Therefore, it should be provided that, unless the Fund board specifically votes to do otherwise, Fund investments in any year should be sufficient to make total automatic drawing rights grow by an agreed percentage. The chosen figure should be designed to make total world reserves, including gold as well as IMF credits, expand along with world trade and production.

Simultaneously, the usefulness of automatic drawing rights on the Fund could be increased by making them directly transferable between members. At present they can be shifted from one member to another only with the intervention of the somewhat cumbersome currency-drawing procedures of the IMF.

As just outlined, the proposal does not solve the transitional problem of consolidating existing dollar balances. This too could be done by the Fund, through an initial purchase of dollars from the countries now holding them. Or, it could be done separately, outside the IMF, by funding our current short-term dollar debts into long-term debts payable in the other country's currency. The attractiveness of this funding could be enhanced by providing that the lending country could cash them early, with the United States, another country, or the Fund, in case it encountered balance-of-payments difficulties of its own.

The proposal for Fund investment in a package of national currencies and World Bank bonds has obvious kinship with the CRU idea. But it avoids the disadvantages of the CRU. It is located in an established worldwide organization, and all countries share in its benefits. It does not replace existing dollar balances in a manner unfair and injurious to the U.S.; this consolidation must be separately managed. The IMF investment proposal is flexible and it does not have a deflationary or restrictive bias.

The creation of international money, for circulation among central banks, is entirely feasible. The institutional setting for this development already exists in the International Monetary Fund. The way is there; what is needed is the will. Progress is blocked, on the one hand, by French distrust of money creation in the IMF and, on the other hand, by U.S. insistence on the sanctity of the dollar's status as a reserve currency. In my view, the U.S. should now be willing to accept an orderly consolidation of dollar balances in return for new arrangements to provide reserves through the IMF.

The United States no longer has blank check privileges, and official holders of dollars are restless and unhappy. Nevertheless the U.S. government continues to insist that we will consider no reform of international monetary arrangements that threatens the reserve-currency position of the dollar. This insistence has contributed to the current impasse in international discussion of monetary reform. But it has not, of course, prevented the dollar's reserve-currency status from eroding anyway.

The reluctance of U.S. financial circles to accept a solution that recognizes the decline in the reserve-currency status of the dollar seems to be based on a misunderstanding. It is feared that such a solution will also displace the dollar from its role as the principal medium of exchange in private international transactions. This would lose New York and the country some financial business and income, and the nation would no longer enjoy the ability to finance payments deficits from the yearly increment of private foreign demand for dollar working balances.

But no one is proposing to create an international money for private circulation. There the dollar will remain unchallenged, save for the imitative competition of the Euro-dollar. The sources of its advantages, which I tried to explain above, are in no way dependent on the dollar's continued use as an official reserve currency. Indeed, any international monetary reform that removes the danger of a run from dollars into gold can only strengthen the world's private demand for dollars. More important, it can free U.S. policy from our current obsessive concern with gold.

PART V

ACADEMIC ECONOMICS IN WASHINGTON

Chapter 18

Academic Economics in Washington

The Council of Economic Advisers is an outpost of academic economics in the federal government, specifically in the Executive Office of the President. The chairman of the Council and the two other members are usually university professors on leave. Many of the fifteen to twenty economists who make up the Council's professional staff are likewise borrowed temporarily from academic careers. What function does such an academic outpost serve? Is this a good way to organize professional advice? These questions are by no means unique to economics, for economics is only one of the complex and technical fields where the President of the United States needs disinterested professional advice in meeting his immense responsibilities. Organizing advice for the President in nuclear physics and other natural sciences involves many of the same problems and even bigger stakes.

Everyone is familiar with recurrent complaints against the alleged influence of impractical, newfangled theorists who have never met a payroll or carried a precinct. (For some reason, professors serving Republican administrations are generally spared these attacks.) I believe, with natural bias, that the government gains from harboring an enclave of academic economists on Pennsylvania Avenue. On their side, university administrators and department chairmen—though they respond with generosity, pride, and tolerance when specific faculty members are called to service in Washington—sometimes feel, after a cumulation of

This essay, originally published in *Ventures* (Yale University Graduate School, Winter 1963), reports my reflections after returning to Yale from service as a member of President Kennedy's Council of Economic Advisers, 1961–62.

such drafts, that tours of duty with the government divert professors from their real missions. I believe, however, that in most instances experience in Washington will enrich future teaching and research with a heightened sense of relevance and with new insights into the policy-making process.

The Council of Economic Advisers was established by the Employment Act of 1946, which declares it to be federal policy to promote "maximum employment, production, and purchasing power." The central job of the Council is to help the President keep track of current and foreseeable trends in employment, production, and purchasing power and to compare the actual and probable levels of these variables with the "maximum" objectives of the Act. The Council must assist the President in reporting to the Congress at least once a year his view of the state of the economy and his recommendations for achieving the purposes of the Employment Act. The President makes an Economic Report every January, at about the same time as his Budget Message. The Economic Report is considered and appraised by the Joint Economic Committee of the two Houses of Congress, also created by the 1946 Act.

The Council is, therefore, a part of the machinery set up by the Employment Act to implement a solemn but somewhat vague declaration of national policy—a declaration which could easily, without effective machinery, be a nonoperational statement of pious intent. The Council's statutory *raison d'être* is to serve as the President's intelligence arm in the eternal war against the business cycle. But in fact, the Council's field is much wider. At least under the Kennedy Administration, it embraced almost all questions of economic policy that came to the White House. In all probability something like the Council would have been set up even without the Employment Act. For the President needs—along with the many other considerations and viewpoints which guide his decisions on a host of complex issues—the opinions of *full-time professional advisers who are an integral part of his Administration but not of any Cabinet Department.* A similar need is met by the Bureau of the Budget, which brings to the surveillance of federal expenditures and departmental programs both expertise in details and the perspective of a *Presidential* agency. Recently another similar need has led to the creation of the Office of the Science Adviser, like the Council a point of contact between universities and the Presidency.

What can professional advisers of academic background contribute on economic issues? Whether the subject is unemployment, taxation, the Federal budget, postal rates, gold, sugar quotas, mergers, tariff protection, or interest rates, the professional economist should be able to bring to both the making and the explanation of decisions certain distinctive talents. He is trained to look at things from the standpoint of the economy as a whole as against sectoral interests, to look for ultimate and remote consequences as well as immediate and superficial effects, to worry about the great mass of silent consumers as well as highly vocal and visible producers, to examine the mutual consistency of diverse policies, to appeal to statistics and history but to handle them with care and respect, to question traditional definitions of issue and to challenge assumptions of policy that otherwise are taken for granted, and to seek alternative solutions which might reconcile conflicting objectives with less cost and inefficiency. It is important that this training and outlook be represented high in the councils of any Administration, though obviously there are quite different viewpoints which are at least equally relevant.

Why full-time advisers? Cannot the academic economist's contributions be made by part-time, ad hoc consultations? The answer is no, for several reasons. The docket is much too heavy. No occasional consultant can be effective on the whole range of issues, and an uncoördinated stable of consultants will not have any consistent overview or policy line. On most issues, there is a great body of statistical information and a long history of intragovernmental debate and negotiation, available only inside the government; the uninitiated academic who ignores this material is likely to be ignored himself or laughed out of court, however righteous his cause. An academic expert certainly can be effective as an occasional consultant, but he needs the support and focus of an established government agency. Very often the Council can serve as a base, but only because the Council economists are themselves on full-time duty.

Why must professional advisers be an integral part of the

President's Administration? Some observers have wished the Council to be coldly scientific and nonpolitical, offering purely "objective" diagnoses and recommendations to the President and to other political officers, and avoiding identification with policy decisions. The first Chairman, Edwin B. Nourse, tried to steer the Council in this direction. But he did not succeed, and for very good reasons. One reason, of course, is that economic policy-making is by no means an exact and objective science. (And neither is scientific policy-making, for that matter—witness the disagreements among physicists about the facts, to say nothing of the ethics, of nuclear testing.) But the main reason is this: To be at all effective, the Council must be identified with the President and his Administration. If the Council is to take an important and active part in the process of argument, persuasion, and compromise by which policy decisions are made, it must feel in the same measure as other participants joint responsibility for the decisions. A neutral nonpartisan Council, if one could be imagined, would simply not provide advice of interest to the President. The President needs professional advice, and he needs disinterested advice. But he needs to get it from people who, he knows, generally share his objectives and his concern for the record of his Administration. No adviser expects to have his counsel accepted always. A professional economic adviser, in particular, will understand the reasons of legislative and political feasibility and strategy that compel his advice to be rejected or diluted in many cases.

The Council is sometimes criticized for being "political" and "partisan," for compromising the purity and objectivity of academic learning. But economics has always been a policy-oriented subject. Unless it is applied to the urgent policy issues of the day, it will become a sterile exercise, without use or interest. Those who fear that economics will be discredited if it is applied remind me of a football coach who never plays his star back for fear he might be injured.

There is, of course, a potential danger that advisers will be used simply to justify and embellish policy decisions they have no part in making. The ultimate protection against this danger is resignation, as it is for any official who finds himself consistently in conflict with the whole direction of Administration policy. A second protection is confidentiality of advice. This tradition is, in fact, important both for the President and his advisers. The President could be unfairly embarrassed if it were known that he rejected the Council's advice in this or that instance, or that some particular Presidential policy was the Council's brainchild. For this very reason, if its advice to the President were public, the Council would be under pressure to tailor its analytical diagnoses and policy recommendations to Administration decisions already taken for other reasons.

Why does the President need professional economic advisers outside the Cabinet Departments? In Britain and France, for example, the functions performed by our Council of Economic Advisers are performed within the ministries corresponding to our Treasury. Obviously, the Secretary of the Treasury—and to a lesser degree his colleagues in Commerce, Labor, and Agriculture—have powerful voices in determining the economic policy of any Administration. Obviously, too, these and other departments and agencies need and in fact use the services of professional economists. But if the economist's viewpoint is going to be expressed to the President only through Cabinet Secretaries, it is going to be muffled. Every department has its own parochial interests, determined by the specific responsibilities assigned to it by the Congress and by its particular constituencies outside the government. We do not have cabinet government of the kind which is associated with a parliamentary system. We have, in effect, within the executive branch as well as among the branches of the federal government, a system of checks and balances. That is why effective Presidential leadership would be very difficult without the Executive Office of the President (of which the major component is the Bureau of the Budget).

The Executive Office is the natural locus for an agency like the Council of Economic Advisers. It gives the Council a position half in and half out of the White House. This enables the Council to speak independently of the various departments, which of course often have divergent views. At the same time the Council chairman and members are not White House assistants proper, with the responsibility of trying to look at all problems through the President's eyes, reconciling conflicting views within the Administration, and balancing all relevant considerations, including those of political strategy and Congressional relations. This relieves the Council of a job for which academic economists would not be particularly well-suited and permits the Council to concentrate on the substance of its task. It also permits the Council to play a role in public education on economic issues that would not be open to members of the White House staff.

Finally, what of the effects on the universities of manning this academic outpost in the government? I think that any academician who has had this experience will come away from it with two feelings about his own profession: confidence and humility. He will have confidence that analytical economics can make a valuable and distinctive contribution to policy; it can raise significantly the level of the considerations of logic and of fact which go into policy discussions and decisions. He will have humility because he will have noticed many instances where decisions had to be based on incomplete information, inadequate research, and hasty analysis. He will return to his university, then, with a new sense of research priorities and with an enriched agenda of problems for himself, his colleagues, and his students.

Index

Africa, 61
Agriculture: and federal controls, 6–7, 32–33; and prices, 118–19; and inflation, 130–31
American Medical Association, 41
American Telephone and Telegraph, 52
Anderson, Robert, 141, 142
Antitrust laws, 6
Arrow, Kenneth, 106
Asia, 61

Balance of payments, 12, 13, 163, 179–80; and unemployment, 46; and Gross National Product, 76; deficit, 143; and international monetary system, 151, 154–60, 172–73; and exchange controls, 171
Bank of International Settlements, 163
Benson, Ezra Taft, 32
Bretton Woods Agreement, 161, 162, 164, 165, 174, 181–82, 183
Britain. *See* United Kingdom
Budget, federal, 7–8, 11, 21, 26–27, 36; balanced, as principle, 37, 38–40, 71–72; and economic stabilization and national priorities, 45; deficit and surplus, 49–55, 87
Bureau of the Budget, 203–04
Burns, Arthur F., 29
Business community and economy, 8
Byrd, Harry, 58, 61–62, 64

Canada, 158, 166, 171; and monetary union with U.S., 192
Capital: exports of U.S., 158–59; markets and controls, 159
Civil defense, 60
Classical economics, economists, 57, 64
Collective Reserve Unit, 152, 194–95, 197
Commission on Money and Credit, 27
Committee for Economic Development, 8, 11, 37
Common Market, 76, 172
Congress, U.S.: Joint Economic Committee of, 10, 135, 138, 142–43; and Federal Reserve System, 136–37
Constitution, U.S., 8–9
Consumption, 72–73; and economic growth, 79–88, 108
Controls, 33–34; and planning, 5–6, 11, 12–13; direct (wages

and prices), 6, 117, 123–24, 126–27, 137, 141; indirect (fiscal and monetary policy), 7–9, 13, 118, 119, 124–26

Council of Economic Advisers, 9, 13, 38, 119, 201–06

Credit and inflation, 129

CRU. *See* Collective Reserve Unit

Debt, national, 61–62

Defense Production Act of *1950*, 117

Defense spending, 42; and budget, 40, 45–46, 58–69; domestic economic consequences of, 70–74, 123; international economic consequences of, 70, 74–77

Deficits and surpluses, non-government, 49–55. *See also* Budget, federal, deficit and surplus

De Gaulle, Charles, 120, 144, 152, 186, 190–91, 194

Denison, Edward F., 107

Depression of *1929–32*, 36–37, 38, 52, 57, 94, 144–48

Détente, Cold War, 41–42

Dollar, U.S., 75–77, 120–21, 140–41, 143, 147, 153–60, 174, 178–79; and Depression of *1929–32*, 146; as reserve currency, 186–92, 197–98

Drug legislation, 6

Dulles, John Foster, 58

Education, 79

Eisenhower, Dwight D., Administration of, 3, 8, 12, 13, 26, 27, 39, 45, 67–68, 71, 79, 119, 141; fiscal policies of, 57–69;

and Federal Reserve System, 137, 138

Employment Act of *1946*, 9–10, 12, 26, 27, 38, 39, 41, 72, 202

Euro-dollar, 188–89, 198

Europe and postwar economics, 75–77

Exchange rates, 161–62, 164, 165–66, 171, 174–75, 180–83, 191

Federal Reserve Act of *1913*, 9

Federal Reserve Banks, 9

Federal Reserve System, 12, 27, 28, 118, 119, 125, 134–43, 144–46, 170, 185, 188–89; and "tight money," 66–67; decisions political or technical, 139

Fiscal policy, 139–40, 169; and "fiscal responsibility," 39; and foreign policy, 58–63

Foreign aid, U.S., 158

Fowler, Henry, 152

France, 8, 11–12, 16, 37, 75, 76, 147, 165, 192, 194–95, 197; Bank of, 178–79

Friedman, Milton, 25–26, 27–28, 129

Germany, 8, 16, 37, 65, 192

Gold, 177–85; standard, 28, 146–47, 152; exchange system and the dollar, 190–91, 198

Goldberg, Arthur, 13–14

Goldenweiser, E. A., 136

Goldwater, Barry, 3, 25–34, 40

Government, federal: and business, 15–24, 25–26, 33, 35–36; measurements of size of, 30–32; and states, 32; economic role of, 35–42, 56–69;

U.S., European attitudes toward, 38
Great Britain. *See* United Kingdom
Gross National Product, 7, 42, 79; origin and destination of, 18, 22; and federal government, 19, 21–24, 30–31; and defense, 47, 70, 71; and research, 74; *1953–59*, 80–82; and private investment, 80–83
Growth, economic, 11–12, 79–88; rate of, 65; and allocation of output, 78–88; and capacity, 90–92; and unemployment, 92–94; and international politics, 94–96; and Gross National Product, 96–97; and military power, 95; and consumption, 98–101, 108; and federal government, 99–104; and intertemporal choice, 101–04, 107, 109; and private capital markets, 104–07; and monetary policy, 144–48

Harris, Seymour, 152
Heller, Walter, 29
Holland, 8, 13
Hoover, Herbert, 36, 37, 57
Humphrey, George, 26, 39, 58, 59, 61, 64, 68, 141, 142

Inflation, 8, 13, 41, 61, 72; sources and kinds of, 65–67; and monetary policy, 87, 117–27; "gap" and "income," 123–25; and unemployment, 128–33; and purchasing power, 129; and U.S. balance of payments, 157–58; -deflation cycle, 159

Insurance, old age, 18
Interest Equalization Tax, 158
Interest rates, 120, 124–26, 140, 144, 146, 168–71; time preference set, 91, 100, 111; technological set, 91, 110; international level of, 159
International Monetary Fund, 152, 163, 185, 189, 194, 195–97
International monetary system: automatic and discretionary corrective mechanisms for, 162–63; liquidity and payment imbalances, 164–65; and employment, 166–67; and price levels, 167–68; and internal monetary policy, 168–69; and exchange controls, 171–72; and government transactions, 172–73; and markets, 173–74; and exchange rates, 174–75. *See also* Money, international
Investment, 79; government and private, 23–24; private, and economic growth, 80–87
Italy, 16

Japan, 16, 65
Johnson, Lyndon B., Administration of, 3, 29, 32, 40–42, 58

Kennedy, John F., Administration of, 3, 5, 27, 29, 33, 41, 42, 73, 134, 135, 136, 138, 139, 202; and federal economic control, 5–6, 10, 14; and growth rate, 11–12; and balance of payments, 12; and steel prices, 13–14; and business community, 15, 18, 24,

39, 40. *See also* Government, federal: and business
Keynes, John Maynard, Keynesian economics, 6, 36–37, 38, 146, 147
Khrushchev, Nikita, 58
Knowland, William, 58

Labor: and business, 19; and inflation, 129–33
Lanzillotti, Robert F., 108
Latin America, 61
Lippmann, Walter, 42
Low Countries, 37

Marshall Plan, 157
Martin, William McChesney, Jr., 58, 67, 120–21, 136, 140, 141, 144–48
Marxist economics, 36–37
Medicare, 18
Monetary policy, 8–10, 11, 27–28, 38, 85; and inflation, 117–27, 135–40; and direct controls, 137, 141; and unemployment, 137–40; and economic growth, 139–41; and federal debt, 137, 141–43; and reserve requirements, 142; and international agreements, 143. *See also* International monetary system
Money, international, 176–85; and liquidity, 184–85; and the dollar, 186–92, 197–98; and gold standard, 192–93; and Collective Reserve Unit, 194–95, 197; and International Monetary Fund, 195–98. *See also* International monetary system
Monopolies, 6

National Security Council, 136
Nationalization of industry, 17
New Deal, 3, 5, 15, 35–36, 38, 39; as non-Keynesian, 37
Nixon, Richard M., 13
Non-purchase transactions of government, 21
Norris, George, 17
Nourse, Edwin B., 204

Organization for Economic Cooperation and Development, 163

Phelps, Edmund S., 108, 110
Physiocrats, 64
Planning, 9–10, 14; and controls, 5–6, 7, 11, 12–13
Productivity: and budget, taxes, 62–65; and wages, 130–33; and investment, 169

Recessions of *1958, 1960,* 39
Research, effect on growth rate, 79
Reserves, 179–85. *See also* Dollar, U.S.; Money, international
Revenue Act of *1964,* 29
"Right-to-work" legislation, 131–32
Rockefeller, David, 23
Roosevelt, Franklin Delano, 36, 37, 39, 57, 146. *See also* New Deal
Rueff, Jacques, 144, 152, 190, 193

Scandinavia, 37
Schumpeter, Joseph, 161
Slichter, Sumner, 125
Smith, Adam, 57, 64
Snyder, John, 135, 141

Social Security Act of *1935,* 18, 86
Socialism, 18
Solow, R. M., 108
South Africa, 193
Southeast Asia, 42
Soviet Union, 16, 60, 62, 63, 69, 156, 178, 193, 194
Steel prices, 13–14, 40
Sterling, 187
Stock market and economy, 146
Supply and demand, 7
Sweden, 8
Switzerland, 16; franc, 187

Taft-Hartley Act, 131
Taxes, 7, 8, 10, 62; and investment, 11; reform in, 20; reductions in, 24, 26–27, 28–30, 40–41, 42, 53–54, 73, 93, 169; and capital assets depreciation, 39, 40; and productivity, 64–65; and private investment, 85–86; and consumption, 86; increases in state and local, 86; and economic growth, 86–87; and expense deductions, 86–87; and inflation, 118, 123–24; progressive, 128–29
Technology: and economic growth rate, 99–100, 108–10; and labor, 132–33
Tranche, gold and "credit," 195–96

Transfer payments, 7
Transportation industries, 7
Treasury, U.S., 12, 103, 118, 157, 169–70, 184–85; and Federal Reserve System, 135, 141–43
Triffin, Robert, 144, 179
Truman, Harry S., Administration of, 5, 15, 38, 39, 135, 141

Unemployment, 36–37, 79, 87; insurance, 10, 41; and public capital expenditures, 10, 41; and tax reductions, 41; and investment incentives, 46; and inflation, 124, 128–33; and monetary policy, 137–40, 145, 147, 153, 166–67
United Kingdom, 8, 11–12, 16, 37, 65, 75, 171; monetary policy of, 126; and gold standard, pound, 146–48
United States Steel Corporation, 14
Utilities, public, 6

Wages and prices, 13, 34, 128–32
War: Korean, 42, 59, 117, 118, 123, 124, 129, 138; Second World, 6, 117, 118
Wilson, Charles E., 58, 59, 61

Yugoslavia, 16